A Woman's Journey through Esther

8 Lessons on Faith Exclusively for Women

Dee Brestin

FAITHFUL Woman™

For Her. For God. For Real.

faithfulwoman.com

Titles by Dee Brestin

From Cook Communications

The Friendships of Women
The Friendships of Women Workbook
We Are Sisters
The Joy of Women's Friendships
The Joy of Eating Right
The Joy of Hospitality
A Woman of Joy
A Woman of Value
A Woman of Insight
A Woman's Journey through Luke
A Woman's Journey through Ruth
A Woman's Journey through Esther
A Woman's Journey through 1 Peter
A Woman's Journey through Psalms
My Daughter, My Daughter

From Harold Shaw/Waterbrook

Proverbs and Parables
Ecclesiastes
Examining the Claims of Christ (John 1–5)
1, 2 Peter and Jude
How Should a Christian Live? (1, 2, 3 John)
Higher Ground
Building Your House on the Lord
Friendship

From Word

Falling in Love with Jesus

Find Dee on the net: www.DeeBrestin.com

Faithful Woman is an imprint of
Cook Communications Ministries, Colorado Springs, Colorado 80918
Cook Communications, Paris, Ontario
Kingsway Communications, Eastbourne, England

Unless otherwise indicated, all Scriptures are from the *Holy Bible, New International Version.*® Copyright © 1973, 1978, 1984 by International Bible Society. Used by permission of Zondervan Publishing House. All rights reserved; other quotes are from J.B. Phillips: *The New Testament in Modern English* (PH), Revised Edition,©J.B. Phillips, 1958, 1960, 1972, permission of Macmillan Publishing Co. and Collins Publishers; and the *Authorized (King James) Version* (KJV).

Editors: Barbara Williams and Dorian Coover-Cox
Design: Bill Gray
Cover Photo: Kevin Buckley

Contents

How I Thank God For:

My Editors:
Dorian Coover-Cox, who teaches Old Testament at Dallas Theological Seminary, for her knowledge, discernment, and perspective as a godly woman.

Barb Williams for her diligence with every jot, tittle, and comma.

My Brothers in Christ at Cook Communications Ministries:
especially and always, Greg Clouse.

Bill Gray, for such striking covers for this series.

My Assistant:
Gay Tillotson, whose energy, enthusiasm, insight, and administrative skill have made us an Ecclesiastes 4:9-10 team.

My Sisters in Christ, Including:
the reflective and diligent women of Sonrise Bible Study who tested this guide and vulnerably allowed me to read their answers.

My prayer support team to whom I attribute the wonderful sense I have had of God's hand upon me.

My Family, Including:
all of our children for their prayers and support.

and my absolutely amazing and godly husband, Steve, who is so supportive, encouraging, insightful, and dear.

Introduction

Two books in the Bible are dedicated to women whose lives made an enormous difference: Esther and Ruth. Should we not, as women, be studying them in depth?

SISTERS, PLEASE HEAR THIS:

THE BOOKS OF ESTHER AND RUTH ARE GOD'S SPECIAL GIFTS TO US.

TREASURE THEM! UNWRAP THEM SLOWLY.

ALLOW HIS SPIRIT TO ETCH THEIR TRUTHS UPON YOUR HEART.

The primary message of Esther is that *God's unseen hand guides our lives.* In studying Esther, you will be stretched to become a DETECTIVE FOR THE DIVINE, to see God's hand, not only in Esther, but in your everyday life. Just as He led Esther, He longs to lead you. Our first lesson will look at this exciting theme of God's providence.

In addition, Esther has some particularly encouraging messages for women. Through the Book of Esther I have heard my Heavenly Father say:

Do you want to be a part of a dynamic women's ministry? Esther had one of the most successful ministries in history when she learned to do it My way.

I care about you. Even if you have failed Me, I love you. I long for you to walk closely with Me. If you are facing enormous difficulties because of your own sin or simply because of sin in the world, I long to help you. I can bring beauty out of ashes.

I created you uniquely as a woman. Because of your relational gifts, you will have an enormous impact on the men, women, and children in your life. You can either walk in the flesh, as Haman's wife, Zeresh, did, and reap destruction on your loved ones, or you can walk in the Spirit, as Esther learned to do, and bring salvation to your loved ones.

I am here and I am not silent. The world you live in is far from Me, and at times I may seem far away as well. Many believers do not have Me as their first love. But I long to bring revival to your heart, My daughter, to make you a shining light, a STAR (Esther means "Star") in the midst of a crooked and depraved generation.

Esther may be one of the most challenging books you have ever studied. You may question the choices of the individuals. Was Vashti right to disobey her husband? Was Esther right to take part in a beauty contest that involved sleeping with the king? When the tables were turned at the close of the story, were Mordecai and Esther right to order the slaughter of over 75,000 men? You will not find editorial comment in the Book of Esther, as you usually do in Scripture. When David committed adultery, when Miriam murmured against Moses, God made His displeasure known. Here, in Esther, God seems strangely silent. The book is told with severe restraint, without even the mention of God. Why?

Many believe that because this book was written about the Jews in a secular kingdom, it needed to be told with restraint. Yet believers reading it would discern the hand of God.

Another explanation, given by F.B. Huey, Jr., in *The Expositor's Bible Commentary,* is that "the hiddenness of God can sometimes be explained as evidence of His displeasure" (Amos 8:11, Ezekiel 11:23).[1] The Jews living in Persia had chosen to stay in this worldly land, rather than return to the Holy Land, when they had been given the opportunity fifty years before. John Brug believes the book is deliberately written in the style of a Persian secular narrative "to reflect the point of view of a person living outside of the Holy Land in an unholy heathen kingdom. . . . The secular tone of the book reflects the conditions and attitudes of Jews scattered in Persia, rather than those of pious Jews in the Holy Land."[2]

This guide will challenge you to continually hold up the choices of the individuals in Esther to the light of Christ. Esther is challenging, but that is good for us. We will hear different views on this book from the pulpit and from commentators, and we need, as with everything we hear, to be like the Bereans who searched Scripture to see if what they were hearing was true (Acts 17:11).

Mordecai and Esther were real people like you and me, living in a world that was obsessed with materialism, sexual immorality, entertainment, prejudice, pride, and revenge. Often, it seems, they were like the world around them. Yet there are also some golden moments when they rose above the decadence and walked by faith.

Though God's name is not in the Book of Esther, His fingerprints are everywhere. It gives me great hope to see how God did not forsake His people, even though I am convinced their behavior grieved Him. It is because of God's mercy that we are not consumed. I have often failed my Lord. I am a chipped pot, and yet I long to be used. Will He ever give up on me? Not as long as I keep coming back to Him. Not as long as I allow His gentle hands to put me over the heat so that He can mend me, mold me, and make me a vessel fit to be used.

Instructions for Preparation and Discussion

When Esther's heart became right with God, He used her mightily to impact others. I am praying you will be obedient to God so that He can impact this small group through you.

1.   Do your homework at the same time and in the same place daily and you will establish a habit. *Expect* God to speak to you personally through His Word. Then, when you come to study, it will be with an overflowing heart rather than an empty cup. What richness you will therefore experience together as sisters in Christ!

2.   Get a hymnal, as hymns will be suggested to enrich your quiet time. A prayer journal would also be an excellent additional tool. Effective prayer warriors take a few minutes each day to jot down their prayers and then highlight or star the answers.

3.   Be sensitive in discussion. The naturally talkative women need to exercise control and the shy women need to exercise faith and speak up. Esther learned when to speak and when to be silent. May you as well.

4.   Stay on target in the discussions. These lessons can be discussed in ninety minutes. If you don't have that much time, you have two options:

   A. Divide the lessons. Do three days a week for sixteen weeks. Do that week's prayer exercise both weeks.

   B. Do the whole lesson but discuss half the questions.

5.   Follow the instructions for group prayer at the close of each lesson. Keep confidences in the group. When Esther and her maids fasted (and we assume, therefore, prayed) God worked mightily. There is power when women pray together.

IF GOD BE WITH US, WHO CAN BE AGAINST US?

Esther said, "The adversary and enemy
is this vile Haman." Then Haman was
terrified before the king and queen.
—Esther 7:6

$\mathcal{O}$ne

Providence

$\mathcal{A}$n unseen hand guiding us. That is providence. Mysterious, but sovereign. Merrill Unger defined providence as "the continual care which God exercises over the universe which He has created."[3]

Francis Schaeffer said: "He is there and He is not silent."[4]

Providence explains why the guards at Ravensbruck allowed Corrie ten Boom, with a Bible hidden on her person, to pass untouched while they ran their hands thoroughly over all who passed before and after her.[5]

Providence explains the desire of the Christian men in Charlotte, North Carolina to hold an all-day prayer meeting in a pasture "which happened" to belong to Frank Graham (who had a young son named Billy). That day one of the men, Vernon Patterson, prayed that "out of Charlotte the Lord would raise up someone to preach the Gospel to the ends of the earth."[6]

And it is faith in the providence of God which brought Joni Eareckson Tada, paralyzed by a diving accident, to peace. Like Job, she cried out with the deepest, darkest questions. Did she receive an answer? Yes, an answer similar to the answer Job received from God. Joni summarizes it with Romans 11:33-36:

> *Oh, the depth of the riches of the wisdom and knowledge of God! How unsearchable His judgments, and His paths beyond tracing out! Who has known the mind of the Lord? Or who has been His counselor? Who has ever given to God, that God should repay him? For from Him and through Him and to Him are all things. To Him be the glory forever! Amen.*

Joni says that if God *had* answered her questions more specifically, "It would have been like dumping a water tower into a Dixie cup. My poor pea brain wouldn't have been able to process it."[7] But she knows He cares, He is in control, and He does all things well in His time. That is providence.

God's care for the world is also revealed in His plan, heralded by the prophets. In this lesson you will read how Jeremiah foretold that the Jews would be taken captive by Nebuchadnezzar of Babylon for seventy years. And just as Jeremiah foretold, it happened. You will read how Isaiah said that God would use Cyrus, even though Cyrus didn't acknowledge God, to free the Jews and allow them to return to the Holy Land. And just as Isaiah foretold, it happened.

Yet though God has a plan, somehow, in the mysterious workings of God, our choices still make a difference. In this lesson you will see the choices that Daniel and his three young friends made in Babylon and the impact those choices had in glorifying God. Generations later, Esther was faced with a similar situation and made a different choice, a choice which I believe did not honor God. However, even when we fail God, He is able to bring good out of the situation. He is the Redeemer! He is the Master of bringing beauty out of ashes. He still cares, He is still in control, and He still does all things well in His time. That is providence.

Prepare Your Heart to Hear

In this first lesson you will read difficult prophecies and see their fulfillments. This will give you a foundation for the Book of Esther, but it will also be challenging for you. So each day, before you begin, ask God to help you. He is eager to do so.

Memory Work

This week you will memorize Romans 11:33, which provides a wonderful context for the Book of Esther and which will help you as you walk with a mysterious God.

> **Oh, the depth of the riches of the wisdom and knowledge of God! How unsearchable His judgments, and His paths beyond tracing out!**

Warm-Up

Share your name and why you came to this group.

Share one impression, if possible, that you have about Esther. Or, answer this: If Hollywood were to produce a movie about Esther, whom might they cast as the breathtaking heroine?

Day 1: Preparation

The opening introductions are vital, so read them carefully.

1. Comment on what stood out to you from the:

   A. The Introduction (pp. 5–7)

   B. The Instructions for Preparation and Discussion (p. 8)

   C. The Introduction to Chapter One: PROVIDENCE (pp. 10–11)

Spend five minutes on the memory passage.

Often doing a word at a time will help to cement it in your mind:
Romans
Romans 11
Romans 11:33
Romans 11:33 Oh,
Romans 11:33 Oh, the
Romans 11:33 Oh, the depth
etc.

A helpful but optional exercise this week will be to read through the Book of Esther as an overview.

(Optional) Read Esther 1 and 2.

2. In a sentence, describe what happened in these chapters.

Day 2: A Detective for the Divine

Because the central theme of the Book of Esther is God's providence, you are going to become a DETECTIVE FOR THE DIVINE in your everyday life. "The Chapel of the Air," a national radio program, introduced what became an enormously popular spiritual discipline which they called "The God Hunt." During the fifty days before Easter, individuals were encouraged to hunt for ways they could see God at work in their lives. Likewise, we are going to do a version of the God Hunt for the next forty-eight days. Each day you will reflect on the last twenty-four hours and become a DETECTIVE FOR THE DIVINE. The most typical ways to appreciate the Presence of God are through:

A. HIS WORD.
Did He increase your understanding or love of Him? (If so, how?) Did He speak to a particular need in your life through the passage? (If so, how?)

HIS WORD

B. HIS PRESENCE.
Did you come into His Presence? Think of your quiet time with God as opening the drapes on a window. When did you sense the drapes opening? (Was it as you sang a particular hymn? Was it when

HIS PRESENCE

you stilled yourself and realized that He is God? Did you sense Him guiding you as you planned your day's priorities? Was it as you read over your prayer journal and realized He had answered a prayer?)

C. HIS PROVISION.

This can be any blessing, as every good gift comes from God (James 1:17). (Jot down some of the gifts one is apt to take for granted: a sunset, a baby's smile, healthy eyes.) Or, perhaps you sensed unusual means or evidence of grace, as we sense in Esther. (If so, *what* made you wonder if God might be involved? Was a friend's visit particularly timely? Did the same idea occur to three of you as you prayed together?)

HIS PROVISION

3. How may God possibly have provided in the following passages?

A. Mordecai, a key figure in the Book of Esther, was going to need to be in favor with the king. See Esther 2:21-23.

B. Esther realized that if she went into the king without being summoned that she might be put to death. See Esther 5:2-3.

C. Esther was planning to ask Xerxes for mercy toward her family, which included Mordecai. See Esther 6:1-2.

4.   Share, in a sentence, a time when you sensed God's hand in your life through His Word, His presence, or His provision. What made you think God was involved? (If you tend to share the same incident, try to think of a more recent one.)

Review your memory work.

(Optional) Read Esther 3 and 4.

5.   In a sentence, describe what happened in these chapters.

Detective for the Divine

Have you sensed God in the last twenty-four hours through:

A. His Word? (If so, what did you learn?)

B. His Presence? (If so, when?)

C. His Provision? (If so, what? Why do you suspect God?)

Day 3: One Hundred Twenty Years before "Esther"

Over a century before the events in the Book of Esther occurred, the pagan King Nebuchadnezzar of Babylon raided and eventually destroyed Jerusalem. He took many Jews to Babylon. Among them were Daniel, Shadrach, Meshach, Abednego (605 B.C.; Daniel 1:1-4) and Mordecai's great grandfather Kish (597 B.C.; Esther 2:5-6; 2 Kings 24:8-16).

6.   One way we see the hand of God is through His plan, which He often revealed ahead of time to the prophets. Jeremiah warned the Jews that King Nebuchadnezzar would besiege Jerusalem. What did He say in Jeremiah 25:1-14?

7.   How do you see Jeremiah's prophecy fulfilled in Daniel 1:1-8?

8.   How do you see Jeremiah's prophecy fulfilled by the history given concerning Mordecai's ancestors in Esther 2:5-6?

(Optional) Read Esther 5.

9. Describe what happened in this chapter in a sentence.

Review your memory work.

Sing "Immortal, Invisible" in your personal quiet time in praise to God. (It will be in most hymnals.)

Detective for the Divine

Have you sensed God in your life in the last twenty-four hours? (His Word, His Presence, His Provision) If so, how?

Day 4: Godly Believers in a Pagan World

Daniel and his three young friends faced enormous pressure to hide their faith and to engage in the immoral practices planned by King Nebuchadnezzar. I believe it is important to see this, for the believers in the Book of Esther are faced with similar pressures and respond quite differently, at least initially.

Read Daniel 1:3-5.

10. Which young men were chosen to serve the king and how did they prepare?

Compare Esther 2:2-4 and 2:12.

11. Which young women were chosen to serve the king and how did they prepare?

Read Daniel 1:6-21.

12. What step of faith did Daniel and his three young friends take?

How do you see God at work in their lives in this passage?

Read Daniel 3.

13. What immoral act did Nebuchadnezzar ask of the Jews?

What step of faith did Shadrach, Meshach, and Abednego take? What did they say in Daniel 3:17-18?

How do you see God at work in their lives in this passage?

(Optional) Read Esther 6.

14. Describe what happened in this chapter in a sentence.

Detective for the Divine

Have you been aware of God in your life in the last twenty-four hours? If so, how? (One of the ways God reveals Himself is through His Word. See Psalm 119:18, 33-38.)

Day 5: Fifty Years before "Esther"

Just as Jeremiah prophesied, after seventy years of captivity, the king of Babylon was punished. (This all occurred between 539 and 536 B.C.) The Persians, led by Cyrus, overran Babylon. Cyrus gave the Jews the freedom to choose to go back to Jerusalem or to stay. Many devout Jews went back to Jerusalem, but most of the Jews stayed. Many commentators, such as J. Vernon McGee, believe that those who stayed were out of the will of God.[8]

Two hundred years before Esther, Isaiah prophesied that Cyrus, who had not even been born, would free the Jews. Fifty years before Esther, Isaiah's prophecy was fulfilled when Cyrus freed the Jews.

Providence. God cares. God has a plan. God is in control.

Read Isaiah 44:21 through Isaiah 45:13.

15. In Isaiah's prophecy, what do you learn about:
    A. God's feelings for His people? (Isaiah 44:21-22)

    B. God? (Isaiah 44:24-26; 45:5-7, 9-12)

    C. Cyrus of Persia? (Isaiah 44:28–45:5, 13)

16. God may use those who do not acknowledge Him. (He can use stones if He chooses.) What does Proverbs 21:1 teach?

17. What do you learn from the above passages about God's involvement in the world He created?

Read Ezra 1 and 2.

18. How do you see the fulfillment of the prophecies God gave to Jeremiah and to Isaiah through the opening of Ezra?

The large tomb of Cyrus still exists in what is now Iran. Though the inscription is now unreadable, Plutarch (A.D. 90) quoted it as having said: "O man, whosoever thou art and whencesoever thou comest, for I know that thou wilt come, I am Cyrus and I won for the Persians their empire. Do not, therefore, begrudge me this little earth which covers my body."[9]

(Optional) Read Esther 7 and 8.

19. Describe in a sentence what happened in these chapters.

Review your memory verse.

Detective for the Divine

Have you seen God in your life in the last twenty-four hours? If so, how? (One way is through His presence. See Philippians 4:6-7.)

Day 6: Even When We Fail Him, God Does Not Forsake Us

The Book of Esther is a mysterious book, not only in the fact that God's name is not mentioned (though His hand is evident) but in the behavior of God's people. Many commentators question the moral behavior of Mordecai and Esther, a subject we will return to repeatedly. As you read the closing bloody chapters, you may wonder about that as well. If you read various commentators, you will find three points of view:

1. Defense and adulation of Mordecai and Esther. Many feel that because they are in the Bible, they must be models of virtue. (Several times, when I have raised the question of Mordecai's or Esther's character in my speaking, I have had women who were absolutely outraged!)

2. Complete condemnation of Mordecai and Esther.

3. Seeing their strengths and their weaknesses, holding their behavior up to the plumb line of Scripture.

I prefer the realism of the third. Certainly Scripture is clear that God's people often fell short of His standard. Just because God uses someone (as we saw in the case of Cyrus) it does not mean all of his behavior is a model for us. I agree with F.B. Huey, Jr., who says:

Criticism of the morality of Esther and Mordecai is no more an attack on the inspiration of the Scriptures than a condemnation of the idolatry of the Israelites during the monarchy is an attack on the Scriptures.[10]

Understanding this impacts how we see not only the Book of Esther, but all of Scripture. Before we assume someone is a positive role model, we should be aware of a didactic Scripture (teaching Scripture) to support his or her behavior. For example, both David and Solomon had many wives. But can you think of a teaching, as would be found in the words of Jesus or Paul, which supports polygamy? Can you think of one that refutes it? (Matthew 19:4-8 helps us to see that God's plan is for one man and one woman for one life.) Therefore, even though David was a man after God's heart, his polygamous lifestyle is not to be imitated.

I have come to realize that just as Mary, the mother of Jesus, has become too important to some Christians, so has Esther become almost an icon of worship to others. In part that springs from our tendency to worship people instead of God. I believe it may also be a result of our Judeo-Christian heritage. When the Book of Esther is read at Purim, the children boo when Haman's name is read and cheer loudly each time the name of Esther or Mordecai is mentioned. Considering the enormous suffering of the Jewish people, it is understandable that Esther, who risked her life for her people, would be a heroine. And she is, indeed, a heroine. Yet even heroes and heroines have feet of clay. One woman said to me, "When I heard you speak on the Book of Esther and you asked us to consider whether or not Esther may have succumbed to immoraltiy in her youth, I was shocked and offended. All during my childhood Esther was presented to me as the perfect woman. I had trouble listening to you with hearing ears. But, in time, I have come to realize that I am wading into treacherous water when I expect any person to be perfect. People can be models to us, but only God can be our foundation." As that wonderful old hymn, "The Solid Rock," says, "I dare not trust the sweetest frame, but wholly lean on Jesus' name."

Don't be afraid to hold the behavior of Esther or Mordecai up to the plumb line of Scripture. Don't be devasted if they don't always measure up. No person should ever be worshiped. God alone is worthy of worship.

Even when Esther and Mordecai were out of God's will, God still cared for them. What hope that gives me, His erring child!

In your personal quiet time, sing "The Solid Rock."

Read 1 Corinthians 10:1-13.

20. Why might God give us negative examples in Scripture according to verse 11?

How can we know if a biblical character is behaving in a way that is pleasing or displeasing to God if the passage itself does not tell us?

(Optional) Read Esther 9 and 10.

21. In a sentence, describe how the Book of Esther closes.

22. How have you seen the truths of Romans 11:33 in this lesson?

What has particularly impressed you?

Detective for the Divine

Have you seen God in your life in the last twenty-four hours? If so, how? (One of the ways God shows His love is through His provision. See Matthew 6:26.)

23. What incidence of God's working in your life stands out to you from this week? (Give women freedom to pass.)

Prayer Time

This week, the discussion leader will close in prayer.

Two

The Tides of the Times

Though the events in Esther's life took place long, long ago (twenty-five centuries ago) and far, far away (Persia stretched from India to Greece and from Egypt to Ethiopia), the values and the empty pursuits of people sound just like the values and the empty pursuits of our world. The opulent world into which Esther was swept mirrored the decadent world we live in, a world obsessed with wealth, power, entertainment, youth and beauty, sexual immorality, and alcohol.

The Book of Esther is one of the few books of the Bible that takes place outside of the Holy Land. It was difficult for a believer to live in the decadent world of Persia and not be pulled down. How relevant to us today!

It isn't easy to live in this world and not be of it. It isn't easy to maintain an eternal perspective when everyone around us, even many believers, has the "under the sun perspective," the perspective that focuses on the visible and loses sight of the invisible.

The secret to being steadfast in a world of strong tides is to be anchored to the Lord and His Word. It is imperative for us who live in a "contemporary Persia" to cling to that anchor with all of our hearts, with all of our souls, and with all of our minds. It is imperative for us to relinquish the false gods, to stop running to television, food binges, or the praise of man for our sense of well-being, but to run instead to the Lover of our souls, our Lord Jesus.

Prepare Your Heart to Hear

Before each of the following six devotional times, determine to listen to the Lord. The world shouts, but God whispers. So be still and listen.

Memory Work

Though you might not see it yet, there are golden nuggets in Esther 4:12-16 that will transform your life. If you hide it in your heart, it will help to keep you flying above the decadence of this world long after this study is over. This week begin with Esther 4:12-13.

> **When Esther's words were reported to Mordecai, he sent back this answer: "Do not think that because you are in the king's house you alone of all the Jews will escape."**

Memorizing a word at a time will seal it in your mind:
    Esther
    Esther 4
    Esther 4:12-16
    Esther 4:12-16 When
    Esther 4:12-16 When Esther's
    etc.

Warm-Up

Share a transitory dream (something that you would like, though you know it will pass away, like a new sofa or luxuriant hair) and an eternal dream (something that will not pass away, like a ministry in line with your gifts or the salvation of a loved one). Be concise. (Give women the freedom to pass.)

Day1: Overview

God longs for us to set our affections on things above, for that is our real life. The transitory things, the seen things, are passing away. The things that matter are the unseen things—and they will never pass away.

1.   The world in which Esther lived was obsessed with the seen, with the transitory. What do you learn from the following passages?
    A. Romans 12:2

B. 2 Corinthians 4:18

C. Colossians 3:1-10

2.   Solomon was a believer, yet he ignored God's warnings and lost his eternal perspective. Caught up in the mind-set of his world, the "under the sun perspective," he ran after transitory things. Describe his pursuits and how they affected him in Ecclesiastes 2:1-11.

We are half-hearted creatures, fooling about with drink and sex and ambition when infinite joy is offered to us, like an ignorant child who wants to go on making mud pies in a slum because he cannot imagine what is meant by the offer of a holiday at the sea.
C.S. Lewis[11]

3.   As you examine your own life, is Jesus your first love? When you wake up in the morning, are your thoughts drawn to Him? Are you eager to run to Him, to feast on His Word? What do you think about? What do you talk about?

4. Comment on what stood out to you from the Introductory notes to this lesson (p. 27)

Spend five minutes on your memory passage.

In your quiet time sing "Seek Ye First" and "As the Deer."

Detective for the Divine

Have you sensed God in the last twenty-four hours through:

A. His Word? (If so, what did you learn?)

B. His Presence? (If so, when?)

C. His Provision? (If so, what? Why do you suspect God?)

Day 2: The Playboy of the Persian World

The Book of Esther begins with a six-month party! Can you imagine? This party was probably a military planning session. Xerxes wanted not only to plan the strategy for his war with Greece, but also to impress the leaders of his provinces with his wealth and power. So he put on an ostentatious display of wealth and what J. Vernon McGee describes as "a perpetual smorgasbord."[12]

Xerxes was King of Persia. Your Bible might call him "King Ahasuerus" which really refers to his Persian title rather than his name. His Greek name is Xerxes and the Greek historian Herodotus describes him as "impatient, hot-tempered, and lecherous."[13] He was the grandson of Cyrus the Great (the Persian king who freed the Jews fifty years earlier) and the son of Darius. Darius had suffered a humiliating defeat by Greece, and his son continued the effort to extend the Persian Empire to include Greece.

At the end of his six-month party, Xerxes threw a seven-day drinking party. (This was a stag party. The queen was having her own party in another part of the palace.) As happens with things "under the sun," the party was getting boring. His judgment impaired by wine, Xerxes made a foolish decision in an attempt to end the gala with a bang. He decided to parade his lovely wife Vashti before this tipsy and lustful crowd.

The ancient historian Josephus says that all Vashti was to wear was her royal crown, that she was to appear in the nude.[14] Another historical source, Jonathan ben Uzziel, concurs.[15] Whether or not they are correct, it is clear it was a demeaning request, like asking Vashti to pop out of a cardboard cake.

But Vashti refused to come. SURPRISE! All that money and effort spent to convince the military leaders that Xerxes was quite a guy and the party ends instead with the humiliation of Xerxes. The lights don't go on. The curtain doesn't go up. The queen will not obey her husband.

Read Esther 1:1-12.

5. Xerxes had two banquets. The first was a feast and the second, the closing seven days, a drinking party that was meant to be a grand finale. What was the purpose of all this according to verse 4?

What are some of the ways he accomplished this? (Describe the furnishings, the goblets, and the atmosphere.)

Joyce Baldwin comments on the difference between the opulent Persian palace of Xerxes and the lean life of most of his subjects. Then, as now, most people in western Asia had hard lives and food was none too plentiful. The palace at Susa was elevated 120 feet to emphasize the supremacy of the king.[16]

6. Using a dictionary, define *eunuch*. Define *castrate*.

   How does this practice show the darkness of the times? The attitude toward people?

7. Describe the frame of mind of Xerxes in Esther 1:10.

   Describe his plan for a grand finale. Include the command, the purpose, and the number of eunuchs asked to implement it.

8. Why do you think Xerxes ordered seven eunuchs to bring one woman?

Perhaps the eunuchs were going to carry Vashti in on some sort of a platform. W. Dinwiddie, in *The Pulpit Commentary*, writes:

> *The emphatic way in which the number and names of the chamberlains are given seems to indicate that there was some fear of the queen in the king's heart. He knew her character, and was not unconscious of the insult implied in his command. . . . He perhaps hoped by this parade to overcome any objection she might have to obey his strange command. But the quality of evil is not affected by the garnishings with which men clothe and try to conceal it.* [17]

9. How did this planned finale show the darkness of the times? The attitude toward people?

10. Based on what you have seen so far, describe Xerxes and his perspective of life. (Include what was important to him, the value he placed on people, and anything else you can discern from the text.)

Xerxes mistreated the poor, the helpless, and women. He was obsessed with wine, wealth, and entertainment. All that mattered to him was his own selfish agenda and status. Believers also can be swept up by the tides of the times if they are not clinging to God and His Word.

Sing "In My Life, Lord, Be Glorified" in your personal quiet time.

Ask God to help you be honest with the following questions.

A. Does my life show that I care for the poor and the helpless? If so, how?

B. Does my life show that I value women equally with men, as God does? If so, how?

C. Does my life show that I am anchored to God through the time I spend with Him and the way I spend that time?

D. Are there false gods to whom I am running for comfort? (A new home, a package of Oreos, romance novels?) Why should I run to God instead?

Detective for the Divine

Has your love or understanding of God grown in the last twenty-four hours? If so, how?

Day 3: An Angry King

Xerxes is well known in secular history for his temper. Many feel he suffered from some sort of abnormality (as has been true of many leaders such as Nebuchadnezzar, Napolean, Hitler, Saddam Hussein) that revealed itself in hysterical fits of rage. One incident is reported by several historians. Xerxes took a fleet of 300 ships to Salamis in an attempt to conquer Greece. (This probably occurred after this party.) All 300 ships were destroyed by the waves and Xerxes had the sea whipped for the offense!

The historian Herodotus reports on an incident which shows the enormous callousness of Xerxes. Pythius of Lydia, rumored to be the second-richest man on earth, offered to finance Xerxes' war with Greece. Pythius had five sons who would be serving in the war and Pythius requested a small favor. Could the eldest son remain at home to care for his aging father? In a rage, Xerxes gave orders to have this eldest son cut in half. The two halves of the son's body were placed on either side of the road and the army marched out between them. Xerxes said to Pythius: "There, now you can keep your son at home."

Joni Eareckson Tada and Steven Estes, in *When God Weeps*,[18] comment on the above incident and make the contrast between Xerxes, who had no compassion for his subjects, and God, who was willing to be "cut in half," so to speak, to die on a cross, that we might live.

Research shows that one of the strongest male drives is for status. (This drive can be used by God to help a man accomplish good things. However, if a man does not find his identity in Christ, status can easily become the god of his life.) Xerxes had an overwhelming drive for status. Archeologists have uncovered Xerxes' palace at Susa and have verified the accuracy of the opulence described in Esther 1:6.[19] Inscriptions have also been found in which Xerxes referred to himself as "the great King, the King of Kings, the King of the lands occupied by many races, the King of this great world."[20]

Is this a man you would dare embarrass publicly?

Read Esther 1:10-22.

11. After his humiliation, whom does Xerxes consult? What do you learn about them from Esther 1:13-14?

Considering Xerxes' temperament, what kind of counsel would you expect his advisers to give him? Explain.

12. Describe Memucan's counsel and reasoning (Esther 1:16-20).

13. What do you learn about the laws of the Medes and the Persians? (Esther 1:19)

14. At what point in this story is "Queen" omitted from Vashti's name? Do you see any significance?

15. Comment on Memucan's logic (Esther 1:16-18).

16. Describe the hysteria in the court and the backlash to Vashti (Esther 1:16-22).

Comment on how effective you think Memucan's law would be in causing women to respect their husbands. How would it have affected you?

The key to respect is not a demand, it is a demonstration. It's love, it's honor, it's looking out for the needs of your wife, it's helping your wife to grow in faith. . . .

Radio Pastor Woodrow Kroll[21]

17. What causes you to respect a man?

Personal Action Assignment

Is there a man in your life whom you respect and could encourage? Write him a note telling him the things you see in his life which cause you to respect him. (Do this right now—it can be a brief note.)

Whom did you write? Would you be willing to share anything you said?

Review your memory verse.

Detective for the Divine

Have you seen God at work in your life in the last twenty-four hours? If so, how? (Review the ways described on pp. 13–14.)

Day 4: Vashti, the Queen Who Said "No"

Historically there is some confusion on the identity of Vashti because Xerxes had many wives and concubines. Amestris is the name of the queen in historical records and many believe that Vashti and Amestris were the same woman.

Amestris, historians tell us, was cruel and vengeful. Once, when Xerxes tried to seduce his brother's wife, Amestris had the woman horribly mutilated.[22] Records also show that Amestris buried people alive who fell out of her favor.[23]

However, some believe Vashti and Amestris were two different women. Rabbinic records say Vashti was executed after the banquet.[24] If that is true, Amestris might have been queen between Vashti and Esther.

Therefore, we are left to wonder. Did Vashti refuse because she wanted to humiliate Xerxes? Did she refuse because she was a modest and pure woman who would not compromise her standards and come before this drunken stag party? And how did she say no? Gently? We don't know.

What we can try to understand, with the help of didactic Scriptures, is what God asks of Christian wives. (If you are single and think these next few days are not going to be relevant to your life, take heart. You may not always be single, and you may have married friends who would be blessed by your wise counsel.)

Read Esther 1:10-22 again.

18. Give an example of how the author reports the story without commenting on motives.

19. If Vashti was the same historical person as Amestris, what might have motivated her refusal?

20. If Vashti was not Amestris, but a woman of noble character, what might have motivated her refusal?

What Is the Emphasis of Scripture Concerning Marriage?

During the rest of this week we will be considering whether wives should obey their husbands in all circumstances. Anticipate some good discussions in your group as there are two quite different approaches to Christian marriage. One approach is to emphasize authority. (Examples: The Christian Family *by Larry Christenson and* Me? Obey Him? *by Elizabeth Rice Handford.) Another approach is to emphasize relationship. (Examples:* Fashioned for Intimacy *by Jane Hanson and* The Mystery of Marriage *by Mike Mason.) Both approaches have scriptural support. Therefore, a fair question seems to be: What is the prevailing emphasis in Scripture? Is it, "Who is in charge here?" or is it, "The two shall be one"? I am convinced it is the latter and an undo emphasis on the former can distort God's message concerning marriage.*

However, that does not mean that the husband is not the head of the home or that a wife is not called to be submissive. Submission is difficult, for it means dying to ourselves. Scripture makes it clear that wives are called to submit, yet I think you may learn some things in the next few days which will help you tremendously, for these Scriptures are often taken out of context and distorted. It is vital, also, to understand the difference between obedience and submission, a topic we will tackle tomorrow.

For this controversial subject, ask God to lead you into the truth. Be like the noble Bereans and search the Scriptures. Read the upcoming passages carefully, for the real authority is not me or any other Christian author but the author of the Scriptures.

21. What do the following Scriptures teach concerning marriage? Look at the context. Discover all you can.

    A. Genesis 2:24

B. Matthew 19:5-6

C. 1 Corinthians 6:16

D. Ephesians 5:31

22. What prevailing concept do you see in the above passages?

Did you learn anything else? If so, what?

23. In a mysterious way, a marriage in which there is Christian unity reflects the love of God to the world. If you are married, how would those watching perceive the love of God through your marriage?

Review your memory work.

Detective for the Divine

How have you seen God at work in your life in the last twenty-four hours? How has He provided for you in a usual or unusual way? (If unusual, why do you think God was involved?)

Day 5: Should Wives Obey Their Husbands?

Intriguingly, the word "obey" is used in Scripture concerning the relationship of children to their parents and of children of God to their Heavenly Father, but it is not generally used to describe the relationship of a wife to her husband. Instead, the word that is used, in the Greek, is "submit." The one exception occurs in 1 Peter 3:6 where the word "obey" is used to describe the respectful attitude Sarah had toward Abraham. (However, in Genesis 21:12, we also see God telling Abraham to do whatever Sarah tells him to do in regard to sending Hagar away. So even in this example, there seems to be mutual obedience.) Children (and children of God) are told to obey, but wives, with this one exception, are not.

Yet, here, in the pagan setting of the Book of Esther, the hysteria occurs because Vashit did not obey her husband. (And the concept is obedience, though the actual translation is "has not done" rather than "has not obeyed.") When Christ came He elevated wives from a slave/master or child/parent relationship to a co-heir. (See 1 Peter 3:7.) However, though we are not commanded to obey, we are commanded to submit. What is the difference between submission and obedience?

Submission has similarities to obedience, and yet there is a crucial difference. This Greek term, *hupotasso,* conveys a cooperative arrangement. Strong's concordance defines it as "a voluntary attitude of giving in, cooperating." It is a word that is used not only for wives to husbands, but for the whole body of believers, that we might be in harmony. It is an *attitude of humble cooperation that we might be a Christian unity.* J.B. Phillips captures the essence in Colossians 3:18 when he paraphrases, "Wives, adapt yourselves to your husbands, that your marriage may be a Christian unity." This reflects the prevailing emphasis of Scripture which seems to be relationship, or "the two shall become one."

It is possible to obey, yet have a resentful and manipulative attitude that is not submissive or harmonious. God was often angry with the Israelites because though they may have obeyed Him outwardly, their hearts were far from Him (Isaiah 58; Psalm 50). God longs for us as believers to have a humble and gentle attitude toward one another, to have a spirit of cooperation, that our marriages and our relationships in general would be harmonious and thereby glorify Him.

Even "submission" is a foreign concept in a world where everyone wants his own way and does not want to consider the needs of others. Even for a believer submission can be difficult, whether your submission is to a husband, to another believer, or to God. Submission also requires faith, faith that the God we belong to will protect us and care for us when we do what is right. It is a concept that should characterize the behavior of a mature believer, whether male or female, as he or she walks in faith and not in fear.

God's ways are different from the world's ways. It was very helpful for me as a young woman to see that submission is requested of all believers, whether they are male or female. This is a thread that goes through the first letter of Peter, which is intertwined with Peter's thread of living holy lives, doing what is right, and trusting that God will honor us when we do. I think it will be helpful to you to look at this, and then, tomorrow, we will consider what you should do as a wife if your husband asks you to do something that is not holy, as Xerxes did with Vashti.

24. Explain the context of submission in each of the following. Note anything you learn.

A. 1 Peter 2:13-15

B. 1 Peter 2:18-20

C. 1 Peter 2:21-23

In the above passage, note why Jesus was able to submit (1 Peter 2:23) for this is how we can find the power to submit as well.

D. 1 Peter 3:1

E. 1 Peter 3:7

F. 1 Peter 3:8

25. What common reason do you see from the above verses for submission?

26. In Ephesians 5:21 there is a general command to all believers. What is it?

What specific sub-command follows for wives in Ephesians 5:22?

And for husbands in Ephesians 5:25?

And for children in Ephesians 6:1?

27. It is possible to obey outwardly, yet to resist the spirit of submission. God was angry with believers who did this. How do you see this in Isaiah 58:1-4?

28. If you are married, do you have a spirit of humble cooperation with your husband? Do you consider his needs as well as your own? If you are single, do you have this spirit with other believers? When you give up your own way are you bitter or manipulative?

If so, why does this grieve God?

Detective for the Divine

Have you grown in your understanding of God's ways in the last twenty-four hours? If so, how?

In Me? Obey Him? Elizabeth Handford Rice writes: "It seems safe to conclude that Esther was blessed of God because she was obedient, and that Vashti lost her favored position because she refused to obey her husband."[25]

Day 6: When, If Ever, Should a Wife Defy Her Husband?

Vashti refused Xerxes' command. Was she wrong? Some think so. J. Vernon McGee, though he empathized with Vashti's plight, thought she reacted hastily.

She should have considered the fact that her refusal might cause a scandal that would hurt her husband in his position. Under the circumstances she should have gone to the banquet. She should have obeyed the king.[26]

Others commend her. Charles Swindoll says:

I applaud Queen Vashti for her courageous decision. Marriage does not give a husband the right or the license to fulfill his basest fantasies by using his wife as a sexual object.[27]

I respect all of the people whom I have just quoted. We always agree on the center, on who Jesus is and why He came. Yet sometimes believers will disagree on peripheral issues and we must show one another respect and listen to each other with hearing ears. The Book of Esther is particularly difficult because of the absence of editorial comment. It seems impossible to discern Vashti's motives, though I think it is noteworthy that nothing negative is implied about her by the author. However, we can ask a few key questions to shed light on the fog. First, is it right to assume that prosperity or success is always a sign of God's blessing or that suffering is a sign of His displeasure? I believe that is very dangerous, and that didactic Scripture (Scripture which teaches) shows otherwise. (See Hebrews 11:36-40 and 1 Peter 4:12.) Secondly, sometimes a lack of obedience to an immoral request may temporarily embarrass or penalize a husband, but doing what is right is always in his best interest from an eternal point of view. In this situation, I agree that Queen Vashti chose the right road, though I admit we do not know if her motives were pure or impure.

What does Scripture have to say about obedience to immorality? Should a wife set boundaries? Is it permissable for a wife to separate (not divorce) and insist that her husband get help for his abusive or immoral behavior? Some say no, that she needs to obey and trust God. They point to cases in the Old

Testament where a wife went along with a husband's immoral request and God delivered her in the nick of time. (See Genesis 20.) However, again, it is important not to determine principles on the basis of historical examples, for simply because they are in Scripture does not mean they are behaving in a way that was pleasing to God. God uses historical and sometimes even godly people for both negative and positive examples. (Consider David.) Is there a didactic Scripture which tells wives to *obey* husbands in everything, including immorality? No. But there are many didactic Scriptures which tell us to do what is right and which warn us that every person, regardless of gender, will give an account to God.

Those who become hysterical and say that the fabric of Christianity will be rent if wives refuse to obey their husbands' immoral requests remind me of the scene in Esther 1 in which the court was hysterical about Vashti's refusal. Yet I must also balance that by saying that a lack of submission is a serious matter and should not be done capriciously. God is pleased with a gentle and quiet spirit, with a woman who is supportive of her husband. (See 1 Peter 3:4.) We all, because of our sin nature, want our own way. We all, because of our sin nature, fail to look on the other's needs. **The only time I am advocating a lack of submission is when we are asked to submit to sin.**

29. Some say that if a wife obeys an immoral request from her husband that her husband, and not she, will be held accountable. What does Romans 14:12 say?

30. The apostles were told to obey the authorities and to stop preaching about Christ. How did they respond in Acts 5:29?

Abigail, like Vashti, was married to a man who drank too much, had a temper, and made impetuous decisions. First Samuel, unlike the Book of Esther, provides light concerning God's response to the boundaries Abigail drew concerning her husband's behavior.

Read 1 Samuel 25.

31. Record what is told in a sentence in each of the following. Do you discern any editorial comment? If so, what?
   A. 1 Samuel 25:2-3

   B. 1 Samuel 25:4-13

   C. 1 Samuel 25:14-31

   D. 1 Samuel 25:32-35

   E. 1 Samuel 25:36-38

In *Love Must Be Tough,* Dr. James Dobson makes a strong case for a wife standing up to her husband and not enabling his addictive habits with alcohol, extramarital affairs, pornography, etc. Dobson urges her to draw boundaries (perhaps separation) until her husband gets help and shows the fruit of a changed life. Likewise, Dr. Henry Cloud and Dr. John Townsend write in their book, *Boundaries:*

> *We have never seen a "submission problem" that did not have a controlling husband at its root. When the wife begins to set clear boundaries, the lack of Christlikeness in a controlling husband becomes evident because the wife is no longer enabling his immature behavior. She is confronting the truth and setting biblical limits on hurtful behavior. Often, when the wife sets boundaries, the husband begins to grow up.[28]*

32. When, if ever, do you think a wife is free to refuse a request from her husband? Explain your reasoning.

33. Sometimes a woman will cooperate with immorality because she fears the consequences. For example, she may agree to lie to a boss and say that her husband is sick when he is really drunk. How should she respond according to 1 Peter 3:10-14?

In this respect, we can admire Vashti's courage, whether her motives were noble or not. She did what was right, despite the fact that the consequences could have been, and in fact were, severe.

34. How might a woman gently say no, still evidencing a spirit of submission, to, for example, a request to watch pornographic movies or cheat on income tax?

Detective for the Divine

Have you sensed God in the last twenty-four hours through:

    A. His Word? (If so, what did you learn?)

    B. His Presence? (If so, when?)

    C. His Provision? (If so, what? Why do you suspect God?)

35. What incidence of God's working in your life stands out to you from this week? (Give women freedom to pass.)

Prayer Time

Many people are intimidated by the idea of praying out loud. This guide will gently lead you into this gradually. No one will ever be forced to pray out loud.

One of the reasons that the fellowships of women are often warm and encouraging is that God has equipped most of us to be affirming. Giving a blessing to another through prayer is a wonderful gift. Today, stand in a circle holding hands. Each woman will bless the woman on her right in prayer. She might say something like: "Thank You for Linda and her warm smile." If she doesn't know Linda at all, she can say, "Lord, bless Linda." If she doesn't want to speak out loud, she can bless Linda silently and squeeze the hand of the woman on her left, who will be next to give a blessing. (Move clockwise.)

Three

The Contest for the New Miss Persia

The contest involved much more than an evening gown competition. It involved a night with the king (Esther 2:14a). And if Xerxes was not delighted in her, if he didn't summon her by name, she never saw him again (2:14b). She wasn't released to return to her family, nor did she return to the virgins, but she went to live in the house of the concubines (Esther 2:14). Frederic Bush explains:

> It is the king's young body-servants who suggest what he should do to assuage his pathetic regret upon remembering Vashti and her banishment (2:1-2a). Their advice (perhaps befitting their age and experience) is not that he should make an alliance through marriage with one of the powerful and noble families of the regime and so increase the stability of his realm but rather that he should gather beautiful young women from all the provinces of his empire and let the one "who pleases the king be queen in place of Vashti" (2:4). The first criterion for pleasing the king is described with extravagant and derisive hyperbole: their intensive beauty treatment goes on for a full year (2:12)! The second criterion for pleasing him, though told with exquisite reserve, is also transparently clear. "In the evening she would go in, and in the morning she would return again to the harem, but now to the custody of Shaashgaz, the king's eunuch in charge of the concubines. She would not go again to the king unless he took pleasure in her and she was summoned by name" (2:14). . . . the only measure of the woman who is

fit to rule as queen by the king's side is her beauty of figure and face and her performance in his bed![29]

Quite honestly, it distresses me when commentators tiptoe around this chapter and don't clearly condemn the great sin that was committed against hundreds of young women and the families who loved them. I am thankful to men like W. Clarkson, who, in writing about Esther 2, said:

One of the very worst consequences of the reign of sin in this world is the degradation of woman. Meant to be man's helpmeet and companion as he walks the path of life, she became, under its dominion, the mere victim of his ignoble passion.[30]

When I read about hundreds of innocent young women being taken into such a carnal world, I am not only offended as a woman, I am grieved as a mother. We have three precious daughters who value their purity. I cannot imagine how distressed I would be if I had to part from them, knowing I would never see them again, and knowing they were going to be held captive to the sexual whims of a capricious, cruel, sensual despot.

Perhaps many simply miss what is actually going on. Pastor John Bronson of Denver, when speaking on Esther, exclaimed: "Don't you see what is happening here?"[31] Some may not be able to bear to look, for it is depraved. John Brug writes that righteous Jews would have been greatly offended because "the marriage and sexual practices of the Persian court were a far cry from God's intentions when He established marriage."[32] Perhaps believers today have missed what is happening because of the restraint of the author in recording it.

Xerxes and his counselors remind me of Hugh Hefner, the founder of Playboy Enterprises. Hefner has a Playboy Mansion on 5.8 acres where he displays his wealth, complete with flamingos and fabulous gardens. Hefner orchestrates a contest each year to elect the Playmate of the Year and has either lived with or married successive winners.[33]

Prepare Your Heart to Hear
Sing "Open My Eyes, Lord," from your hymnal, each day before you study. Endeavor to meet with God and not just go through the motions of having a quiet time.

Memory Work
Review Esther 4:12-13.

> **When Esther's words were reported to Mordecai, he sent back this answer: "Do not think that because you are in the king's house you alone of all the Jews will escape."**

Warm-Up
Imagine that you were a contestant going through the twelve months of beauty treatments (Esther 2:12). What do you think some of your feelings might have been? (Homesickness, rivalry, fear?) How do you think this atmosphere would impact you?

Day1: Overview
As you read the second chapter of Esther, carefully observe the tides of the times. What are the pursuits? The values? The treatment of women?

In the midst of this chapter we are introduced to our hero and heroine, Mordecai and Esther. There are diverse opinions concerning their behavior. Some theologians applaud them, others raise their eyebrows. Before you come to your own convictions, record whatever you see that seems praiseworthy. Record whatever you see that seems to fall short of God's standard.

Read Esther 2.

1.   What do you see that reveals the values and pursuits of the leadership of the Persian kingdom? (Give verses.)

2.   What do you see that seems praiseworthy in Mordecai or Esther? (Give verses.)

3. What do you see that may not be?

4. Comment on the Introductory notes to this lesson (pp. 50–51).

Review your memory passage.

Detective for the Divine
Have you seen God at work in your life in the last twenty-four hours? If so, how? (He speaks through His Word. See Psalm 19:8.)

Day Two: The Search for Beautiful Young Virgins
An extensive search was made for beautiful young virgins. Commissioners were appointed to find them in every one of the 127 provinces over which Xerxes reigned, an area bigger than the United States.

God values virginity in the unmarried, and we should as well. Since a woman can give her virginity to only one man, it is a priceless treasure. Joyce Baldwin speaks of the horror that must have been caused by the roundup of these girls.[34] As a mother, I would be heartbroken to have a daughter taken like this. To me it would be akin to the horrible time when Herod's troops came through to kill the male babies under two years of age.

How many virgins were rounded up? Josephus, an ancient historian, estimates 400.[35] Paton speculates that one virgin a night for four years (Esther 1:3; 2:16) would have been 1,460 young women.[36] However, the contest may not have lasted four years, for historians believe that during much of the time between his third and seventh year of reign Xerxes was away battling Greece. (The historian Herodotus says Xerxes came home defeated and consoled himself with his harem.) The "Later" or "After these things" with which chapter 2 begins may refer to the war with Greece.

Read Esther 2:1-4.

5. What does the author tell us about King Xerxes in Esther 2:1?

If Vashti was still around and Xerxes could bring her back, why might that be a problem for the counselors?

6. Describe the proposal that the counselors make to Xerxes.

What is your impression of Xerxes' counselors? Explain.

How does Xerxes respond to this plan?

7. Explain how the following passages show the honor God places on virginity.
A. Genesis 24:15-16

B. Deuteronomy 22:13-21

C. Song of Songs 4:12

8. Another reason the virgin bride is precious in God's sight is because she symbolizes the purity He longs for in us. How does 2 Corinthians 11:2 show this?

9. Whether we are single or married, the Scripture is clear we are to remain pure sexually. What can you do to help yourself stay sexually pure in a sexually immoral society?

Review your memory passage.

Detective for the Divine

Have you seen God at work in your life in the last twenty-four hours? (One way God works is through His presence. See Psalm 34:15.)

Day 3: Introducing Mordecai

Now we are introduced to Mordecai and Esther. Did Mordecai enter Esther into this contest? Some commentators think Mordecai was politically ambitious and entered Esther because he thought she would win. It's possible, but I believe the evidence is strong that Mordecai cared deeply for Esther. In fact, it is a relief to finally come to a phrase showing tenderness toward a woman when the author tells us: "Mordecai had taken her [Esther] as his own daughter when her father and mother died" (Esther 2:7). Mordecai, who was Esther's much older cousin, had taken her in and become like a father to her. There is a tenderness and a respect between them that is evident throughout the book. I doubt therefore that he entered her into such a sordid contest. *The Expositor's Bible Commentary* agrees, saying fathers "apparently did not voluntarily present their daughters as evidenced by the king's appointment of officials to search for the candidates."[37] Likewise, a "tight series of three passive verbs [Esther 2:8] . . . was proclaimed . . . were gathered . . . was taken, portray an irresistible series of events."[38]

However, even if he didn't volunteer Esther, Mordecai does tell Esther to hide her faith. How long did she hide her faith? At least six years. What did that involve? Certainly eating the king's unkosher food (as Daniel refused to do) and perhaps idol worship (as Shadrach, Meshach, and Abednego refused to do). Why did Mordecai tell her to hide her faith? He couldn't have anticipated an edict for a holocaust, but he may have feared anti-Semitism. Mordecai himself, though he lived right in Susa, was not living in such a way that his faith was obvious. Carl Armerding says: "The fact that he had to tell others that he is a Jew is interesting (Esther 3:4). He had lived so long in Persia that he must have become like them."[39] Mordecai falls short when we compare him to Daniel here, but I think he was grieved when they came for Esther. Mordecai paced outside of the palace harem, continually trying to find out how his daughter was and what was happening to her (Esther 2:11). What would have happened if Mordecai had told Esther to refuse? Perhaps she would have been executed, for the times were not friendly to women who said no. Even though he'd lived in Persia a long time, Mordecai must have known it was wrong for Esther to commit sexual immorality and wrong for her to marry a Gentile. But if we are not walking closely with God, when pressure comes, we walk by fear and not by faith, we take things into our own hands because we do not think God will take care of us. I believe Mordecai is afraid and so asks Esther to hide her faith.

J. Vernon McGee says that when you are in God's will you can rest, and he sees Mordecai as out of God's will, pacing up and down, nervously biting his fingernails, wondering how it will all turn out.[40]

Read Esther 2:5-11.

10. What do you learn about Mordecai in Esther 2:5-6?

The phrasing of "who had been carried into exile" (2:6) is confusing, but probably refers to Kish rather than Mordecai, for the exile had begun over a century earlier. The phrasing reflects the strong family solidarity of the Jews: in a sense, Mordecai and Kish were one.

11. What difference do you see between the behavior of Mordecai's ancestors in a pagan land and the behavior of Mordecai in a pagan land? (See Daniel 1 and 3.)

12. Do you think Mordecai entered Esther into the contest? Why or why not?

13. As mothers or mentors, we can encourage our children to be comfortable and safe (but out of the will of God) or to live wholeheartedly for Christ, no matter the cost. What will you do and why?

Detective for the Divine

Have you seen God at work in your life in the last twenty-four hours? If so, how? (One way is through His provision. See Isaiah 40:25-26.)

Review your memory work.

Day 4: Introducing Esther

There was something about her. That cannot be denied. Even her Hebrew name, Hadassah, may have had prophetic symbolism. *Hadassah* means "myrtle," and Joyce Baldwin writes:

> *The myrtle would replace the briars and thorns of the desert, so depicting the Lord's forgiveness and acceptance of his people. Myrtle branches are still carried in procession at the Feast of the Tabernacles, and signify peace*

and thanksgiving. The Persian equivalent, Esther, "star" (cf. Stella), picks up the sound of the Hebrew, and suggests the star-like flowers of the myrtle.[41]

Esther impressed the eunuch in charge of the virgins. Usually the eunuch in this role was "a repulsive old man,"[42] who had political influence. Esther "pleased him and won his favor" (Esther 2:9). The word for "favor" is the covenant word *hesed* and is used again in Esther 2:17. It is an intriguing word in a secular setting and may imply God's hand upon her. (It is the same word used in Daniel 1:9 when we are told God gave Daniel favor.) Another similarity some see with Daniel here is that she showed restraint. Just as Daniel refused the king's rich food, so Esther refused all the garish extravagance in dress and jewelry the other young women were using (Esther 2:15).

14. Discover everything you can about Esther in Esther 2:7-10.

15. *Hadassah* means "myrtle." What associations do you find with myrtle in the following passages? (See their context as well.)
    A. Isaiah 41:19

    B. Isaiah 55:12-13

16. What impact did Esther have on Hegai, the king's eunuch in charge of the virgins?

17. When you think of a woman who wins *hesed,* or favor, loyal love, and kindness with others, what images come to mind?

18. What do you learn about *hesed* from the following passages?
    A. Proverbs 19:22a

    B. Proverbs 20:6

    C. Proverbs 31:26

19. Are you a woman who has received and displays *hesed?* As you are still before the Lord, does He impress anything on your heart?

Detective for the Divine

Have you seen God at work in your life in the last twenty-four hours? If so, how? (Review the ways described on pp. 13–14.)

Day 5: The Contest

Esther, along with the other virgins, had twelve months of beauty treatments. For six months she was bathed and rubbed with oils so that her skin would be soft, touchable, and sweet-smelling for the king. Myrrh was also used for its purifying powers. Another six months were for experimenting with cosmetics. Joyce Baldwin describes some of the practices in Iran and north India, even today, used to prepare a woman for her wedding day. There is ritual cleansing at the communal bathhouse, the plucking of eyebrows and removal of body hair, the painting of hands and feet with henna, and a paste applied to lighten the skin and to remove spots and blemishes.[43] Carl Armerding points out, "Nothing is said about any intellectual or spiritual preparation."[44] Armerding also suspects that the long period for purification must have occurred because the king was considered almost divine, but like many today, the king had "double standards" in that he demanded utmost purity in the girl but had no thought of offering her the same.

Susan Hunt, in *True Woman,* gives historical evidence for women being the primary upholders of virtue. When women fall morally, whole societies collapse. Just or not, moralists have almost always addressed their pleas to women. Alexis de Tocqueville wrote in his classic, *Democracy in America:* "No free communities ever existed without morals, and . . . morals are the work of woman."[45] David Wells, professor of historical and systematic theology at Gordon-Conwell Theological Seminary, writes: "Moralists and campaigners in the nineteenth century almost invariably addressed their pleas and admonitions to women, to the hands that rocked the cradles. Men, it seemed, were beyond redemption unless their women folk could get to them."[46]

Of course, purity for women involves much more than six months of baths in antiseptic oils. It has to do with the heart. Vashti took a stand against the king's decadent behavior and I suspect she deserves our applause. I am sure these virgins knew about Vashti and the price she paid. Perhaps that is why none of them, not even Esther, took a similar stand against the court's sexual immorality.

We are told that each virgin went to spend a night with Xerxes. After her night she did not return to the virgins, but to live with the concubines. Only one could win, and most never saw the king again, unless he was pleased with one and called for her by name (Esther 2:14).

I wonder what would have happened if instead of complying, Esther had gently and humbly taken a stand and said:

I worship the one true God, and before Him, I cannot sleep with a man outside of marriage, nor can I marry a man who worships other gods. If this means my life, then I am willing to die. I mean you no disrespect, O king, but before my God, I cannot do this.

We will never know, because she did not take a stand.

I am sympathetic to the enormous pressure on her. We do not know how old Esther was. She had the poise of a twenty-five-year old, but she may have been much younger, for at that time women married in their early or middle teens. Mordecai, whom she trusted and had always obeyed, told her to hide her faith and participate in the contest. If she was very young, I feel more of the responsibility rests on Mordecai. I am also sympathetic to Mordecai for he loved Esther and probably feared for her life. However, though we can be sympathetic to the enormous pressure upon them, we must be careful that we do not condone their choice. (Once we begin to justify taking the lower road, we are more likely to set foot on the slippery slope ourselves.) I would agree with D. Rowlands who comments that Esther married a heathen, which the Jews were forbidden to do; she became a concubine before she became a wife; and she resorted to duplicity. In reply to the argument that disobedience would bring death, Rowlands writes: "Death is better than dishonour."[47]

20. According to Esther 2:12-14:
    A. Describe the preparation for the night with the king.

Joyce Baldwin says this account reveals "the inhumanity of polygamy" and that though the twelve months of beauty treatments were akin to marriage preparation, "the sad part is that for the majority what awaited them was more like widowhood than marriage."[48]

    B. How long did each virgin spend with the king?

C. After her night with the king, where did she go?

D. Which girls would see the king again?

The passage is loaded with sensual implications, and this Hebrew idiom [translated "to go to, went in to, came to"] is a frequently used OT euphemism for sexual intercourse. . . . Given the frequency with which it is used here, it may well be used with a double entendre.
Frederic William Bush[49]

21. How is the Hebrew idiom "to go to" used in the following?
    A. Genesis 16:2

    B. Ruth 4:13

    C. 2 Samuel 11:4

22. Now find this same idiom in Esther 2:12a, 13a, 14a, and 14c.

What light does this shed on what was happening here?

23. According to Esther 2:15-18:
    A. Whose advice did Esther follow concerning how to adorn herself? Why do you think she did this?

    B. How did those who saw her respond to her? How did Xerxes respond?

    C. Describe the coronation banquet of Esther.

24. Do you think Esther should have taken a stand and refused to participate? Why or why not?

Detective for the Divine

Have you seen God at work in your life in the last twenty-four hours? If so, how? (His Word? His Presence? His Provision?)

What Would Jesus Do?

Is it *ever* right to do wrong? This is a difficult theological issue and I am very aware that I myself will give an account to a holy God for what I teach on this subject.

I do not think that Mordecai and Esther did the right thing in these opening chapters. I also think it is very dangerous, because we have deceitful hearts, to allow ourselves to think that God might lead against His Word. I have a friend who aborted the only child she ever conceived because she thought God was leading her to obey her unbelieving husband. I have another friend who married an unbeliever because he thought that was how God was leading. How easy it is to become confused when the pressure is on! Because the counsel of man and the counsel of our own deceitful hearts is often wrong, we need to be immersed in the pure and trustworthy Word of God.

What do you do, however, when you have to choose between two wrongs? Believers have debated whether or not, for example, it was right for Brother Andrew to smuggle Bibles into closed countries or for Corrie ten Boom to hide the Jews during World War II. In my opinion, these people will be honored for their faith, as Rahab and the parents of Moses were (see Hebrews 11:23 and 31). They were not trying to cling to their own lives, as Mordecai and Esther seemed to be, but instead were risking their lives because they feared God and saw a great wrong being committed against the helpless. Proverbs 24:11-12 gives us God's heart on this:

> *Rescue those being led away to death;*
> *hold back those staggering toward slaughter.*
> *If you say, "But we knew nothing about this,"*

does not he who weighs the heart perceive it?
Does not he who guards your life know it?
Will he not repay each person according to
what he has done?

Some have said, "But isn't this the same as what happened in the Book of Esther?" No, because Mordecai and Esther did not know that in five years there was going to be an edict for a holocaust. I would agree with D. Rowlands who cautions against thinking that their later success justified their earlier actions. If we are going to reason like that, we would have to applaud Joseph's brothers for selling him into slavery or the Jews who crucified the Savior.[50]

It was God who brought good out of the immoral choice of Joseph's brothers. Likewise I feel it was God who brought good out of the immoral choices of Mordecai and Esther. Personally, I find great consolation in the fact that even though they failed Him, God did not abandon them. I do not believe God led them into sin, but it is clear He was still with them. He brings beauty out of ashes. That is why we call Him the Redeemer.

When we ourselves have to face hard choices, we must be aware of how easy it is to be deceived by our own hearts. We must remember the holiness of God and the fact that we will one day have to give an account for our choices.

25. What do you learn about God from the following passages?
    A. James 1:13

    B. 1 John 1:5-6

    C. Psalm 18:24-26

26. According to Jeremiah 17:5-9, why should we not trust in man? Why should we not trust in our own hearts?

Whom should we trust and why?

27. Can you think of a time when you trusted in your own heart and were wrong? If so, what have you learned to keep you from repeating this error?

28. Drawing on wisdom from the following passages, formulate questions to ask yourself when facing difficult choices.
    A. Psalm 119:9-11

    B. Philippians 4:8

C. Matthew 22:36-40

D. 1 Peter 2:21

The question, "What would Jesus do?" from Charles Sheldon's classic In His Steps *is helpful in a decision of ethics. The glorious light of the life of Christ illumines the darkness of our hearts, the counsel of men, and the lies of Satan.*

Review your memory work.

Detective for the Divine

Have you seen God at work in your life in the last twenty-four hours? If so, how? (Have you had an obvious answer to prayer?)

29. What was the most memorable way you saw God work in your life this week?

Prayer Time

The following diagram explains "popcorn prayer."

Four

Darkness and Despair, but God Still Reigns

Even as queen, Esther was still obeying Mordecai and remaining silent about her faith. Mordecai now had a minor political office. (The gate of the city is where legal matters were discussed, as exemplified by Ruth 4.) As he sat at the king's gate, Mordecai overheard Bigthana and Teresh planning to assassinate Xerxes. Mordecai foils the assassination, the eunuchs are put to death, and Mordecai is not thanked or rewarded. But his good deed is recorded in Xerxes' book of chronicles. Years before disaster hit, God was at work.

The little phrase "after these events" (3:1) indicates a passage of several years. We then meet Haman, who had been promoted to the second highest political office. The author mentions that Haman was an Agagite, letting us know that he was related to the ancient enemies of the Jews, which is a crucial clue in understanding the upcoming friction between Haman and Mordecai. Haman's character was revealed clearly by the author. He was a petty man obsessed with pride and the praise of man. Mordecai refused to bow to him. The other officials tried to persuade him to bow, but Mordecai was adamant. Finally the officials went to Haman to point out Mordecai's disrespectful behavior and to announce what Mordecai had revealed to them. He was a Jew! Haman, enraged, "scorned the idea" of executing Mordecai alone. He wanted a holocaust carried out against *all* of the Jews. We see not only the rage of prejudice, but the rage of Satan. Perhaps because the Messiah was to come from the Jews, Satan has always sought to annihilate them, but he never will, for God's hand is on them. When Haman went to Xerxes for permission to carry out this holocaust, his speech was full of half-truths and lies, like the father of lies himself.

Did Mordecai refuse to bow because he had grown in his faith? Was he following the example of his godly ancestors who refused to bow down to the golden idol of Nebuchadnezzar? Certainly Scripture makes it clear that only God is worthy of worship (Revelation 22:9), and the political leaders in Persia seemed to think of themselves as gods. However, there were many godly Jews who bowed down to their political superiors to show respect for the office which God had ordained. The evidence is strong that it was ethnic pride which kept Mordecai from bowing or even rising in Haman's presence (Esther 5:9). Bow to an Agagite? Never. The author does not tell us Mordecai's motive but implies it by mentioning repeatedly that the Jews and the Agagites were enemies. I agree with Bush that this repetition makes it likely that ethnic pride was the motive for Mordecai's refusal to bow.[51]

Haman cast the lot (Pur) to determine the day for the holocaust. Again, in the midst of this horror, we see God's hand. The dice fall on the 13th day of the twelfth month, nearly a year away, giving the Jews time. Though the superstitious Persians saw the number thirteen as unlucky, they felt bound to follow the lot.

Xerxes, characteristically capricious and cruel, signed the edict without even knowing which group he was agreeing to annihilate, for Haman had carefully omitted that detail. As the edict for the holocaust went out, the Persians were bewildered as most didn't share Haman's anti-Semitism. The author also highlights the coldheartedness of Haman and Xerxes, for in the midst of this horror, they sat down to drink (3:15).

Prepare Your Heart to Hear
Before you begin each day, be still and know that He is God.

Memory Work
Review Esther 4:12-13. Continue on with verse 14:

> **For if you remain silent at this time, relief and deliverance for the Jews will arise from another place, but you and your father's family will perish. And who knows but that you have come to royal position for such a time as this?**

Warm-Up

Esther was particularly obedient and respectful of her adoptive father. Share one hint for raising obedient and respectful children.

Day 1: Overview

Sometimes in the midst of distressing circumstances we cannot see God's hand. It is often only in looking back that we see how He was with us.

Sing "In His Time" from your hymnal.

1. Comment on what stood out to you from the Introductory notes (pp. 70–71).

Read Esther 2:19–3:15.

2. What stood out to you that you haven't seen before?

How can you see God's hand in this account?

Spend five minutes on your memory passage.

Detective for the Divine

Have you seen God at work in your life in the last twenty-four hours? (Are you growing in your understanding of God? If so, how?)

Day 2: We're Not Home Yet

Radio pastor Woodrow Kroll tells of a missionary who, after a lifetime of service in Africa, was returning to America on the same ship with Theodore Roosevelt, who had been on a game hunt. An enormous crowd was there for the President with banners, a band, and great fanfare. No one was there to show appreciation for the missionary who had given his life as a servant under primitive conditions. Alone with God, the missionary poured out his feelings about being so unappreciated. Then, in the stillness of his heart, God spoke clearly to him, saying: "You're not home yet."[52]

Though people may not notice the good things you do, though your children and your church may take you for granted, there is One who does notice, and He will be there to welcome you in a way that has never been seen on earth.

Sing "Welcome Home, Children" or "One Day" from your hymnal.

Read Esther 2:19-23.

3. Describe what happens in this passage.

How do you think Mordecai felt when no one thanked him?

When you do something significant for someone and they do not seem to notice, how do you deal with your emotions?

4.   Sometimes parenting can seem like a thankless job, but in time, we do reap, if we don't grow weary. How did Mordecai reap the fruit of faithful parenting? (Esther 2:21)

5.   What do we learn about parenting our children faithfully from the following passages?
   A. Deuteronomy 6:6-9

   B. Proverbs 19:18

   C. Proverbs 22:6

   D. Proverbs 22:15

E. Proverbs 29:15

F. Ephesians 6:4

My husband and I have parented five children. All, by God's grace, are walking with Him. One of the ways God showed us His grace and wisdom was through the many wonderful resources that are available today to help Christian parents train up children in the way they should go. Radio programs such as "Focus on the Family" and "Gateway to Joy" are gold mines. The curriculum, "Growing Kids God's Way," is practical and solid. We read classic parenting books like Dare to Discipline *by James Dobson and* The Blessing *by Gary Smalley and John Trent. And our most frequent form of family devotions was acting out proverbs from the Book of Proverbs, God's parenting manual.*

6.   Even after she was married, Esther obeyed and honored Mordecai. We are commanded to honor our parents all the days of our lives. How could you show your parents honor?

Detective for the Divine
How have you seen God at work in your life in the last twenty-four hours?

Day 3: Haman the Agagite

There was an ancient feud between the ancestors of Haman and Mordecai. The narrator of Esther keeps repeating that Haman was an Agagite, an enemy of the Jews, and that Mordecai was a Jew, and not only a Jew, but also a *Benjamite,* and therefore related to Saul. The narrator of Esther "assumed his readers would recognize the tribal and racial enmity implied by the patronymics of the two men."[53]

Generations before God had commanded Saul to kill all of the Agagites, but Saul disobeyed. J. Vernon McGee says this failure of Saul's almost led to the extermination of his own people, for Haman was an Agagite.[54]

I was a young Christian the first time I read the story of Saul's disobedience to God. I felt I was very busy serving the Lord (volunteering as the church secretary, making bulletin boards in nursing homes, teaching Sunday School), but I had not learned to "hearken." That is, like Saul, I was busy, but I had failed to truly listen to God's still small voice. I *thought* I was serving God but, like Saul, I was actually working at cross-purposes with Him because my plan kept me too busy for His plan! How did God finally get my attention? He brought the story of Saul and the Agagites to me three times in the same day through my quiet time, a sermon, and Christian radio.

I repented of my failure to "hearken." Daily I sought to hear God's still small voice before I served Him. That was a major turning point in the fruitfulness in my Christian life.

Sing "Trust and Obey" or "Be Still and Know" from your hymnal.

Read 1 Samuel 15:1-23.

7. According to 1 Samuel 15:1-23:
   A. What did God tell Saul to do? (1 Samuel 15:3)

   B. What did Saul do? (1 Samuel 15:9)

C. What did God tell Samuel? (1 Samuel 15:11)

D. How did Saul deceive himself? (1 Samuel 15:13)

E. How did Samuel point out his sin? (1 Samuel 15:14, 18)

F. What else did Samuel tell Saul? (1 Samuel 15:22-23)

8.   Do you have your own agenda for serving the Lord? Or are you truly listening to Him?

How does one listen to God?

9.   How does the narrator of Esther identify Mordecai or Haman in each of the following verses?
A. Esther 2:5

B. Esther 3:1

C. Esther 3:4

D. Esther 3:6b

E. Esther 3:10

F. Esther 5:13

G. Esther 6:10

H. Esther 6:13

I. Esther 8:3

J. Esther 8:5

K. Esther 9:24

10. What do you think the author is communicating through the above pattern?

Is there anyone with whom you or your family has an ancient feud? How, according to Ephesians 4:29-32, should you respond?

Read Esther 3:1-4.

11.   Describe what happens in this passage.

12. What is the situation in each of the following passages?
    A. Genesis 23:7

B. 1 Samuel 24:8

C. 2 Samuel 14:4

D. 1 Kings 1:16

13. According to Romans 13:1-2, why are we to show respect for those in authority?

Is it hard for you to pray for political leaders who lack integrity? Why should we, according to 1 Timothy 2:1-4?

14. What caused Mordecai to finally reveal that he was a Jew? (Esther 3:3-4)

Would the people in your community or workplace know that you were a Christian without being told? Why or why not?

15. How did Haman respond when it was pointed out that Mordecai, a Jew, was not bowing down to him? (Esther 3:5-6)

Detective for the Divine

Have you seen God at work in your life in the last twenty-four hours? If so, how? (Review the ways to see God at work in your life on pp. 13–14.)

Day 5: The Edict for the Holocaust

John Whitcomb believes Satan was behind the massacres of the Jews in Nazi Germany. Likewise, Whitcomb says, the "titanic death-struggle of the Book of Esther simply cannot be understood apart from the satanic purposes toward Israel."[55] The astrologers of ancient Persia (see Esther 1:13), the superstitions, and the throwing of the Pur all reveal the hold that Satan had on this pagan kingdom. Yet God is sovereign. We must take heart in knowing that though Satan is the prince of this world, God is mightier, and His will prevails in the end. Though some are astonished that Haman would have been willing to wait nearly a whole year to carry out his pogrom, Whitcomb explains that in the Near East it would be unthinkable to ignore the wisdom of the astrologers or magicians. The fact that Haman was in bondage to Satan's wisdom facilitated the victory of the Jews.

16. What happens in Esther 3:7?

How does this exemplify Proverbs 16:33?

Even the time that Haman cast the Pur seems significant, for it was the month of Nisan, or the month of Passover, the time the Jewish people commemorated their miraculous deliverance by God from slavery in Egypt. (And did you know that Jesus, who freed us from slavery, died on Passover during the hour in which the Passover lambs were slaughtered?)

Read Esther 3:8-11.

17. What truth, half-truth, and lie does Haman tell? (Esther 3:8)

18. How does he bribe Xerxes to agree? (Esther 3:9)

Herodotus explains this was a vast sum, amounting to two thirds of the annual income of the whole empire, a very welcome offer after Xerxes' expensive defeat in Greece. Esther 3:11 might lead you to believe that Xerxes refuses it, but his initial refusal was the beginning of polite Oriental bargaining such as was exemplified by Abraham in Genesis 23. Xerxes took the money as revealed by Esther 4:7 and 7:4.

Read Esther 3:12-15.

19. Contrast the response of the Persians with that of Xerxes and Haman (Esther 3:15).

20. How does Jesus describe Satan in John 8:44?

21. How did Satan use the love of money as a temptation to do wrong in the following situations?
    A. Luke 22:3-5

    B. Acts 5:3

22. Is there an area in your life where the love of money has called you down the wrong path?

Is there a way faith has helped you avoid that wrong path? If so, share.

Review your memory verse.

Detective for the Divine
How has God provided for you in the last twenty-four hours?

Day 6: Put on the Full Armor of God
We may feel like we are battling with evil people on earth, but God tells us our real battle is with Satan. God has given us weapons of warfare, but we must take them out of the closet and put them on, for we are in a war.

Sing "There Is Power in the Blood," "Greater Is He That Is in Me," and "And Can It Be?" from your hymnal.

23. Describe each piece of armor we are to put on and what it represents as explained in Ephesians 6:10-18.

24. If Mordecai and Esther had been armed, how might they have responded differently in the opening of this story?

25. What evil situation are you facing in your life? What have you learned from Ephesians 6 or this lesson which could help?

Detective for the Divine

Have you grown in your understanding of God in the last twenty-four hours? If so, explain.

26. What was your most exciting Detective for the Divine Discovery this week?

Prayer Time

Pair off and pray using the sword of the Spirit. Pray through as much of Ephesians 5:1-22 as time permits for your partner, taking turns on each verse. For example:

Be imitators of God, therefore, as dearly loved children (Ephesians 5:1)
TESS: May Christy imitate and reflect You, dear God.

and live a life of love, just as Christ loved us and gave Himself up for us as a fragrant offering and sacrifice to God (5:2).
CHRISTY: Empower Tess to live a life of love, especially this week with her two children.

But among you there must not be even a hint of sexual immorality, or of any kind of impurity, or of greed, because these are improper for God's holy people (5:3).
TESS: As Christy ministers to college students may her life shine with purity and simplicity.

ᶜ𝒻ive

Predicament, Privilege, and Providence

E sther was comfortably cocooned in the palace when the crisis hit. Now Mordecai urged her out of her cocoon. Her natural response is hesitancy.
Like Esther, Elizabeth Dole was in a position of privilege in politics. Safe and warm, she was not particularly eager to emerge and take the kind of risks that a believer or butterfly might have to face—until she heard a sermon by Gordon MacDonald on Esther 4. She tells the story in *Finding God at Harvard.*[56]

Pastor MacDonald highlighted three themes in Esther 4:13-14. They are: PREDICAMENT, PRIVILEGE, and PROVIDENCE.

When Esther was reluctant to leave her cocoon and go to Xerxes, Mordecai told her that she shared the *PREDICAMENT* of the Jews. "Do not think that because you are in the king's house you alone of all the Jews will escape" (Esther 4:13). "It seems that Mordecai is saying, 'If the thing that stops you from being a servant to thousands of people is your comfort and your security, forget it. You are no more secure in there than we are out here.' Esther shares the predicament."[57] When Elizabeth Dole realized that Jesus was God, she could no longer compartmentalize Him to just one section of her life. If she tried to save her life, if she continued to live for herself, she could lose her soul. This is the predicament we all share.

Mordecai continued: "For if you remain silent at this time, relief and deliverance for the Jews will arise from another place, but you and your father's family will perish" (Esther 4:14). Pastor MacDonald put it like this: "God has given you, Esther, the *PRIVILEGE* to perform. If you don't use that privilege, He may permit you to be pushed aside and give your role to someone else."[58] That was sobering to Elizabeth, for she realized that if she used her privilege for her own selfish goals, for her own career advancement, and not in submission to God, He might take it from her and give it to another.

Finally Mordecai said: "And who knows but that you have come to royal position for such a time as this?" (Esther 4:14) *PROVIDENCE.* Dole writes: "What Mordecai's words say to me is that each of us has a unique assignment in this world, given to us by a sovereign God, to love and serve those within our sphere of influence."[59]

Predicament. Privilege. Providence.

Prepare Your Heart to Hear
What are your daily God-given assignments? Listen, each day.

Memory Work
Review Esther 4:12-14.

Warm-Up
Esther was privileged to have influence with the king. Describe one privileged area of influence to the group. (For example, Bonnie might say: "I'm the high school girls basketball coach and I lead our Fellowship of Christian Athletes group.")

Day 1: Overview
Charles Swindoll says: "This book is not about ancient Persia—it's about us!"[60] I agree. Yet before we can accurately apply this passage to our own lives, we need to understand exactly what happened back then.

Sing "Immortal, Invisible" and "My Tribute" from your hymnal during your quiet time.

1. Comment on what stood out to you from the Introductory notes (pp. 87–88).

Read Esther 4:1-14.

2.   What stood out to you that you haven't seen before?

Review Esther 4:12-14. Is it word perfect?

Detective for the Divine

Have you spied God in the last twenty-four hours? If so, how?
(His Word, His Presence, His Provision)

Day 2: Sackcloth and Ashes

Sometimes the consequences of our actions are astonishingly severe. A lost temper can result in the loss of a precious relationship. A careless moment at the wheel can lead to death.

Joyce Baldwin urges us to imagine that we are Mordecai, "who by his pigheaded pride or loyalty to principle brought disaster not only on himself but his own race."[61] Mordecai tore his clothes, put on sackcloth and ashes, and went out into the city wailing loudly and bitterly. Though this may seem melodramatic to us, it was the way people mourned then, and certainly a bigger crisis cannot be imagined. In every province the Jews were fasting, weeping, and wailing. Many were in sackcloth and ashes. Sackcloth and ashes expressed the kind of grief that would prompt repentance and prayer, though the writer does not mention either.

Esther heard about Mordecai's mourning and was alarmed. It would be as if you heard a family member cry out after receiving news on the phone. You would be frightened and would want to know the reason for the distress.

Esther sent Mordecai clothing, probably so that he could enter the palace and talk to her, for he could not enter the palace in sackcloth and ashes (Esther 4:2). "No lament or sackcloth and ashes must be allowed to disturb the king's merry world of ostentatious pleasure!"[62]

Mordecai refused the clothes. Joyce Baldwin sees his refusal to put on the clothes as discourteous. She writes: "It would nevertheless be in keeping with his awkwardness which caused the crisis in the first place."[63]

Read Esther 4:1-4.

3. Describe what occurs in the above verses.

4. Have you ever done something foolish and were astounded by the severity of the consequences? How did you feel?

5. Describe Jacob's reaction to bad news in Genesis 37:31-35.

How might the grief of the Jews have been similar to the grief of Jacob?

The Jews grieved together. Have you experienced being bonded with others in tragedy? If so, share something about it.

6. Describe the reaction of the Ninevites to Jonah's message in Jonah 3. What was their motive?

Personal Action Assignment

God is pleased when we repent as a nation and when we own the sins of our nation. Spend time in confession to the Lord for your own sins and for the sins of your nation. Some hymns and a praise chorus that might be helpful to you are: "Search Me, O God," "Holy, Holy, Holy," and "Have Thine Own Way."

Detective for the Divine

Did God speak to you through His Spirit when you did the above action assignment? If so, how?

Day 3: Predicament

Now Hathach, a trusted eunuch, began scurrying back and forth between Esther and Mordecai to communicate their messages to one another.

Read Esther 4:5-8.

7. Exactly what did Mordecai tell Hathach?

How long had Esther hidden her faith from Xerxes? (Compare Esther 2:16 with Esther 3:7.) What do you imagine this secrecy involved?

Put yourself in Esther's shoes upon receiving this report and request. What would be some of your emotions?

Knowing what you do about Xerxes from history and Scripture, would you have agreed to go? (It might help to imagine a similar scenario with Hitler.)

Read Esther 4:9-11.

8. Exactly what did Esther tell Hathach?

How often did Esther mention the king? What does this tell you about her perspective?

Kings were protected from being vexed by people problems, but also from attempts at assassination. That is why no one could approach without being summoned. Xerxes was, according to history, eventually assassinated in his bed.

9. Why do you think Xerxes had not summoned Esther for over thirty days? How may she have felt as a result?

10. How did Mordecai urge Esther out of her cocoon in Esther 4:13?

11. How does Jesus urge us out of our cocoon in Matthew 16:24-25?

What application does this have to your life?

In your personal quiet time, sing "Living for Jesus" and "All for Jesus."

Review Esther 4:12-14, making it word perfect.

Detective for the Divine

Have you seen God at work in your life in the last twenty-four hours? If so, how? (Review the ways described on pp. 13–14.)

Day 4: Privilege

Mordecai warned Esther: "For if you remain silent at this time, relief and deliverance for the Jews will arise from another place, but you and your father's family will perish" (Esther 4:14). Most think Mordecai meant that God could still deliver the Jews through another source but that Esther would lose her privilege to be used. Joyce Baldwin says: "God's purposes are not thwarted by the failure of one individual to respond positively to his leading, and the individual is truly free to refuse it, though this leads to loss rather than gain."[64] God is not limited to our willingness to accomplish His purposes. Was Mordecai referring to God? The folksy preacher J. Vernon McGee wrote: "Some day when I see Mordecai (and I will see him), I would like to ask him what he had in mind when he said that deliverance would arise from another place."[65]

Some believe that Mordecai was not referring to God but to a Jewish uprising, for they do not see Mordecai as being a man of faith or piety.[66]

However, though I agree that Mordecai does not seem like a strong man of faith, he still would have been aware of God's promises and care for the Jews. Even the pagans in Persia seemed to have had an awareness of this as seen in Esther 6:13. Mordecai knew God would always have a remnant, but it might not include the Jews dispersed in Persia. It seems to me he was saying, "If you remain silent, God will preserve His people in another time and in another place, but not here in Persia. We will die, Esther!" Or, Mordecai may have meant that God would miraculously deliver the Jews in Persia, but not Esther's family because of her disobedience. In any case, Esther's silence would lead to personal loss for her.

God is not boxed in by a person's disobedience. He may take power from a disobedient believer and give it to an obedient believer, as He did when He took the kingship of Israel from Saul and gave it to David. However, that does not mean that innocent people, including possibly those we love, will not suffer, for they will. God's heart grieves over the disobedience of His people and over the failure of His children to take their positions of privilege seriously.

Many historians have said that there were ample opportunities to stop Hitler early in his reign. Did God call upon a twentieth-century Esther or Mordecai who failed to respond? We do not know. But, as Edmund Burke said in 1776, "The only thing necessary for the triumph of evil is for good men to do nothing."

Begin your quiet time reflecting on the majesty of God by singing "Majesty" and "O for a Thousand Tongues."

12. What promises did God make to the Jews?
    A. Genesis 12:2

    B. Genesis 17:7

    C. Genesis 22:17-18

D. Genesis 28:13-15

13. When God's people were in trouble in the past, God cared and provided. How do you see this in Exodus 2:23–3:12?

What similarities do you see between the predicament and response of Moses and Esther?

14. What message did Mordecai give to Esther in 4:14a?

What do you think Mordecai meant? Explain.

15. What warnings can you find in the following passages concerning a failure to respond to God's call for prayer, repentance, or service?

A. 1 Samuel 2:27-36 and 3:13

B. 1 Samuel 15:22-23

C. 1 Corinthians 9:24–10:13

Personal Action Assigment

Consider God's call upon your life. What talents and spheres of influence has He given you? Ask yourself: Am I taking these seriously? Am I doing what God has called me to do?

Review Esther 4:12-14.

Detective for the Divine

Have you grown in your understanding of God in the last twenty-four hours? If so, explain.

Day 5: Providence

Finally, Mordecai closed with the clincher: "And who knows but that you have come to a royal position for such a time as this?" (Esther 4:14)

If Mordecai was saying that God had led Esther to sleep with the king, marry a Gentile, and hide her faith so that she could one day deliver her people from a holocaust, I disagree, for I am convinced God does not lead into sin. However, I do agree that God is the Master of bringing beauty out of ashes. I think it is possible that God may have caused Hegai and Xerxes to look with favor upon Esther. And now it seems completely plausible that God was calling Esther to take a stand and plead for her people.

Begin your quiet time by meditating on Isaiah 61:3. Then sing: "Spirit of the Living God" and "Immortal, Invisible."

16. What did Mordecai say in Esther 4:14b?

What do you think he meant? Explain.

17. How do the following passages show God working on behalf of His children in difficult situations? And what is His purpose?
    A. Isaiah 61:1-3

B. Romans 8:28-29

18. Think of a difficult situation from your past. (It could have been caused by your own sin or by circumstances beyond your control.) As you reflect, can you see any evidence of God's mercy or hand upon you?

Did any good come out of it? If so, what?

Did you learn anything from it that helped you to be conformed to the image of Christ? If so, what?

Detective for the Divine

Has your reflection on your past brought you to a new awareness of how God may have been working in your life? If so, explain.

Day 6: Encouraging Our Children to Be Brave

One mother tells of her son moving his young family to a large Midwestern city where he took his first job as a structural engineer. One of the first projects he was asked to design was an abortion clinic. He called her, letting her know his brand-new job was on the line if he refused. She empathized with his dilemma but said, "I knew him, and I knew he would do what was right. He just needed encouragement. I told him that even if he lost his job for refusing, God would bless him as He had blessed the Hebrew midwives" (Exodus 1:15-20). Her son took a stand. God gave him favor, he kept his job, and he was then one of the engineers asked to design an exciting project for their state.

Charles Swindoll writes, "As a parent, you have occasions in your life, brief vignettes, little windows of time, where you can step forward and help your children to understand the value of being brave."[67] And if you are not a mother, you are still called to be a mentor and to seize opportunities to encourage the younger women in your path to be brave, to walk by faith, to do what is right—no matter the cost.

19. Why was Mordecai in a unique position to influence Esther?

20. Why do parents sometimes encourage children to seek what is comfortable rather than what is brave or right?

21. Review Mordecai's words in Esther 4:13-14. Remembering the themes of predicament, privilege, and providence, how might you encourage a daughter or young woman to do what is right? Design a short speech based on one of the

following situations: she is facing an unexpected pregnancy; she is choosing a career; or she must choose between denying her Lord and severe persecution.

22. What do you think you will remember from this lesson?

Detective for the Divine

Have you been aware of God in your life in the last twenty-four hours? If so, how?

23. What was your best Detective for the Divine Discovery this week?

Prayer Time

Cluster in groups of three or four and move through the following four topics using the anacronym: ACTS.

A. Adoration, using some of His names for inspiration (the Redeemer, the Word, the Light of the World, the Good Shepherd, the Resurrection and the Life).

C. Confess your sins (audibly or silently).

T. Thanksgiving for ways you have seen God in your life.

S. Supplication (lift a personal need to Him and allow your sisters to support you with sentence prayers).

Six

Out of the Cocoon of Crisis Emerges a Butterfly

*W*hy is this book entitled "Esther"? Perhaps because of her Daniel-like response to Mordecai. After just a moment of consideration she takes a deep breath and says:

> *Go, gather together all the Jews who are in Susa, and fast for me. Do not eat or drink for three days, night or day. I and my maids will fast as you do. When this is done, I will go to the king, even though it is against the law. And if I perish, I perish.*
>
> *Esther 4:16*

Five years before she was afraid to take a life or death stand. Now, out of the cocoon of crisis emerged a butterfly. She prepared for what was going to be one of the most successful women's ministries in history, and we should all take note.

First, she was not going to swim against this raging tide alone. When she did that before she was caught in the undertow with no one to help her. She called for her maids and God's people to fast with her.

I have been privileged to be part of a group of seven women who guide hundreds of women in our town for interdenominational small group Bible studies. The "Sonrise" steering committee together seeks the mind of the Lord on a myriad of decisions involving leadership, materials, and policies. God has blessed Sonrise abundantly, multiplying us from one to seventeen groups, knitting women of various churches together, causing many women to come to the Lord and to grow in Him. He has also blessed the corresponding children's Bible club. When we have a decision of magnitude, we have fasted together to seek the mind of the Lord. Recently we had to fill two vacancies on our board. We prayed and made a list of eight possibilities, women of spiritual depth. Then we agreed to a partial fast (lunches) to seek the mind of Christ. When we came back together God had impressed on each of our minds the name of the same two women for our top choices.

Esther's fast was also corporate, but it was a total fast: no food or drink for three days for anyone. Drastic situations call for drastic measures. How would Xerxes react? He hadn't shown any interest in Esther in over thirty days. He had a cruel temper and had dethroned (and perhaps executed) the last queen.

Still, Esther planned to go to him without being summoned, tell him what she had hidden from him all these years, and plead with him to do something about the terrible decree he had signed. If it didn't go well, Esther and all of her people would die. How's that for a diplomatic challenge?

Prepare Your Heart to Hear
Esther and her maidens sought God's face. Do likewise, daily.

Memory Work
Memorize Esther 4:15-16 over the next two weeks:

> **Then Esther sent this reply to Mordecai: "Go, gather together all the Jews who are in Susa, and fast for me. Do not eat or drink for three days, night or day. I and my maids will fast as you do. When this is done, I will go to the king, even though it is against the law. And if I perish, I perish."**

Warm-Up
Fearful situations can refine us, forcing us to cry out to God for wisdom and the faith to step out. In a sentence, share a time when that was true in your life.

Day 1: Overview

Joni Eareckson Tada said, speaking at Founder's Week at Moody Bible Institute: "God is so uncontrollable! We want Him to be lofty enough to help us in our problems, but not so high that we cannot control Him! God is not safe, but He is good."[68] Joni, who has been paralyzed from a diving accident for over thirty years, knows that God is not safe. But she also knows He is good. She stilled the crowd as she closed by reading from the classic by C.S. Lewis: *The Lion, the Witch, and the Wardrobe.* Aslan the lion represents Christ. Here the children question Mr. and Mrs. Beaver about Aslan.

"Who is Aslan?" asked Susan.

> *"Aslan?" said Mr. Beaver. "Why, don't you know? He's the King. He's the Lord of the whole wood. . . . Don't you know who is the King of Beasts? Aslan is a lion—the Lion, the great Lion."*

> *"Ooh!" said Susan, "I'd thought he was a man. Is he—quite safe? I shall feel rather nervous about meeting a lion."*

> *"That you will, dearie, and no mistake," said Mrs. Beaver; "if there's anyone who can appear before Aslan without their knees knocking, they're either braver than most or else just silly."*

> *"Then he isn't safe?" said Lucy.*

> *"Safe?" said Mr. Beaver; "don't you hear what Mrs. Beaver tells you? Who said anything about safe? 'Course he isn't safe. But he's good."*[69]

Esther could not control God. She knew she might perish, but she would die doing what was right. She is willing to trust Him, for though God is not safe, He is good.

How do we know God is good? The cross is proof.

Begin your quiet time with hymns like "The Old Rugged Cross," "I Will Sing of My Redeemer," and "Worthy Is the Lamb."

1. Comment on what stood out to you from the Introductory notes (pp. 103–104).

2. Comment on what stood out to you from today's Introduction (p. 105).

Read Esther 4:15-5:14.

3. Describe what happens in this account.

What do you see that you haven't seen before?

Detective for the Divine
How have you been aware of God's provision for you in the last twenty-four hours?

Spend five minutes on your memory passage.

Day 2: Fasting in Scripture

Scripture is filled with examples of fasting. Jesus fasted and implied it would be part of our lives ("When you fast . . ."). Historically, great revivals were preceded by fasting and prayer. John Wesley, George Whitefield, Martin Luther, John Calvin, John Knox, Jonathan Edwards, Andrew Murray, and many more fasted regularly to draw upon the wisdom and power of God and to ask for the fires of revival to sweep their land. Fasting has been a neglected discipline in the twentieth century, but it is returning as men like Campus Crusade's founder Bill Bright lead the way in inviting Christian leaders together for times of corporate fasting and prayer. Convinced that America is presently being judged by God, he writes:

> Throughout Scripture, God has made His message clear: "If you obey Me, I will bless you. If you disobey Me, I will discipline you. And if you continue to disobey Me, I will destroy you."[70]

4.   In the following partial list of scriptural examples try to discern the type, motive, and any possible result. Most will be "Normal Fasts" (a day of no food, but water) but a few may be "Partial Fasts" (abstinence from some foods) or "Total Fasts" (no food or water). You may need to read the context as well. If your time is short, do only the passages with stars. Deuteronomy 8:2-3 is the only involuntary fast.

	TYPE	MOTIVE	RESULT
Deuteronomy 8:2-3			
1 Samuel 1:3-11			
2 Samuel 12:13-23			

	TYPE	MOTIVE	RESULT
*Nehemiah 1:3–2:4			
*Esther 4:3			
*Esther 4:16			
*Esther 9:31			
Daniel 1:8-17			
*Jonah 3:5-9			
Luke 2:36-38			

	TYPE	MOTIVE	RESULT
Luke 4:2-14			
*Acts 13:1-3			

5. Summarize what you have learned about fasting from the above.

Detective for the Divine
How have you grown in your understanding of God in the last twenty-four hours?

Day 3: Fasting for Mercy, Power, and Wisdom
Fasting and prayer almost always occur together in the Scripture. Therefore, though prayer is not mentioned in Esther, most believe it occurred. Because the account in Esther is so restrained, we are not told why they fasted, but we can glean purposes by comparing its fasts to similar fasts in Scripture. The fast in Esther 4:3 by the Jews was surely a fast of mourning, but may have been a fast of repentance as well, for the description is similar to the repentant fast of the

Ninevites in Jonah. The fast in Esther 4:16 is reminiscent of Nehemiah's fast, when he needed wisdom and grace before he approached the king. And we are told the fast in Esther 9:31 is a commemorative fast, to help the Jews remember how God turned their mourning into joy.

In the past I have fasted only when I have been desperate. (When our sixteen-year-old son was in rebellion against God, my sister joined me in a fast and we saw God work mightily in John's heart, bringing him fully back to God.) In recent years I am learning the value of fasting at other times, and of the vital importance to God of accompanying any kind of a fast with a pure heart.

A fast can help you to concentrate, putting aside the temporal to seek the spiritual. As women, a large part of our lives may revolve around the preparation of food. When Martha of Bethany wanted Jesus to rebuke her sister because she wasn't helping to prepare His meal, Jesus gently told Martha that Mary had chosen what was best (Luke 10:41-42). Mary, alone among the disciples, realized Jesus was going to die and anointed Him for His burial (John 12:1-8). It wasn't just that Mary had forgotten about food, she was focusing on Christ. In a true fast, we will draw nearer to God, purifying our hearts and discovering His wisdom and power.

6.   What warnings and promises can you find concerning false and true fasts from the following?
    A. Isaiah 58

    B. Joel 2:12-14

7.   If God has blessed you through the discipline of fasting, share something about it.

Review your memory work.

Detective for the Divine

Has God spoken to you through His Spirit in the last twenty-four hours? If so, how?

Day 4: And If I Perish, I Perish

It's such a great line.

Flying home from Thailand with our new twelve-year-old daughter, our fifth child, my husband began to talk longingly of the other children we had seen in Bangkok's orphanage for handicapped children. Steve said, "Some of those little boys were so cute."

Panic began to rise in me. How could I help my husband understand that I had, at least for now, reached my quota of children? A word picture! I thought for a moment and then said,

Honey, please imagine that I am holding on to the airplane wing, clinging by my fingers, praying I do not slip. I want to keep up with you in your Christian walk, but I am afraid I will plummet to my death.

Steve was quiet, absorbing the picture. He put his arm around me. "Dee, is that really how you are feeling?"

I nodded, and then I said:

I am afraid. I don't see how I can adopt more children and survive. But I also want you to know I have given my whole life to the Lord, and if He wants me to adopt more children, then I will.

And if I perish, I perish.

We laughed, and yet that dramatic line did help to communicate my need for support.

Usually you do not perish when you step out into the center of the Lord's will. Usually what you discover is that the road is hard, but God is right there with you. However, unless you are willing to perish, unless you are willing to risk everything to obey God, He will not be able to use you mightily. Radio Pastor Woodrow Kroll said, "I have never known God to fruitfully use anyone who does not come to the 'If I perish, I perish' understanding of life."[71]

Review your memory work.

8. What attitude do you see in the following people and how did God use them because of it?

    A. Esther 4:16

    B. Daniel 3:17-18

    C. Matthew 26:36-42

    D. Acts 4:13-21

9. What attitude are we to have according to the following?
    A. Matthew 16:25-26

B. Mark 8:34-38

10. Describe the "If I perish, I perish" attitude.

Imagine some situations in your life in which it might be revealed whether or not you have this attitude. (Consider not only persecution, but the cost that might be involved in obeying a call of God in career, marriage, etc.)

Do you have this attitude in life? Explain.

In your quiet time sing: "In My Life, Lord, Be Glorified."

Detective for the Divine
Have you seen God at work in your life in the last twenty-four hours? If so, how?

Day 5: Approaching the Dragon One Step at a Time

Charles Swindoll notes that between chapters 4 and 5 in Esther is "white space," a "grand pause" of time.[72] During this time of waiting on God, God pours His wisdom upon Esther, for she obviously has a plan, and a strength from above.

Esther's approach is masterful. She is diplomatic and unrushed. Some think she hesitated because she lost courage. Though she may have been afraid, I do not think that was the reason for her hesitation. I think it was her plan all along to do this slowly, to build suspense, to arouse the king's curiosity. She is walking on faith, one step at a time. Brenda Wilbee, in *Taming the Dragons,* writes,

> *When the king held out his golden scepter she did not immediately fall to her knees and beg for mercy. She approached this dragon one step at a time, asking only for what she felt capable of obtaining.*[73]

11. Record the steps Esther takes in:
    A. Esther 4:16

    B. Esther 5:1

    C. Esther 5:2

    D. Esther 5:3-4

    E. Esther 5:5

F. Esther 5:6-8

By the end of her speech Esther has been able to represent what she wants as a matter of "doing what the king has said" (verse 8), as though it were she rather than he who was doing the favour. D.J. A. Clines[74]

12. What do you learn about approaching difficult situations and how is it exemplified in Esther's approach?

Passage	Teaching	Esther's situation
Psalm 32:8		
Proverbs 16:7		
Proverbs 21:1		
Ecclesiastes 4:9-10		
Isaiah 40:31		

13. What can you learn from Esther in regard to taming dragons?

14. Think of a difficult situation in your life. How do you think God would have you approach it?

One of the most encouraging aspects to me in the Book of Esther is that though Esther failed God in her youth, God gives her another chance to be used mightily of Him. Even if we've blown it (and who of us has not?) God can redeem the purpose of our lives. He can restore the years the locusts have eaten, He can bring beauty out of ashes.

15. What encouragement do you find from God's hand upon Esther?

Detective for the Divine

Have you seen God in your life in the last twenty-four hours through time spent in His Word or in prayer? Explain.

Day 6: The Contrast between Zeresh and Esther

As women we are knit together with those we love and when they hurt, we hurt. If someone hurts my child, my husband, or my dear sister in Christ, I can react like a mother bear. Zeresh shows us how dangerous this is!

Ruthie Thune, wife of the senior pastor of Omaha's Christ Community Church, told me the Book of Esther has made her more aware of her influence over her husband. She told me,

> Sometimes Bob will come home from a church board meeting mildly upset. One of the members has been critical of him or the church. As Bob's main sounding board, I realize that the way I react will have a tremendous impact, not only on him, but on the whole church. If I believe the member's words have merit, I can gently stimulate Bob to consider them carefully. If I become angry as well, I contribute strength to Bob's initial resistance. So I am keenly aware of my need to be sensitive to God's still small voice.

16. How do you feel when a loved one has been upset or hurt by another?

17. From Esther 5:9, list the actions of Mordecai that enraged Haman.

From Esther 5:11-12, list the things Haman boasted about to his wife and friends, noting the order.

What was the fly in the ointment? (Esther 5:13)

18. How does Zeresh respond to the hurt her husband is feeling?

What was foolish about her response?

19. What do you learn about dangerous responses and how is each exemplified in Zeresh?

Passage	Teaching	Zeresh
Proverbs 14:1		
Proverbs 16:18		
Proverbs 26:27		
Romans 12:17-21		
James 1:19-20		

20. What can you learn from the above concerning foolish ways to respond?

Do you see an application to your life?

Detective for the Divine
Has God shown you special mercy in the last twenty-four hours? If so, how?

21. What was your most exciting Detective for the Divine Discovery this week?

Prayer Time
Pair off in twos and pray together.

Seven

If God Be for Us, Who Can Be against Us?

*I*nspired by Esther, our daughter Sally and her friends sought God for a plan to reach their public high school for Christ. They temporarily gave up their school lunches and spent that time in prayer, asking God to impress on each of their hearts the same idea, longing to know His plan and power.

They heard that Campus Crusade's film *Jesus* was coming to the local theater on Easter weekend through the efforts of a few churches. Several had the same idea: "Why not have a special showing just for high school students?" They approached those bringing the film and were given enthusiastic support. However, they also needed their principal's cooperation in order to effectively advertise the event.

Excited, the girls gave up a few more lunches and asked God to show them how and when they should approach their principal and what they should request. By Friday they had their plan. Sally would arrange an appointment with the principal for the following Monday. Then, on Monday, she would go to him and ask permission to put up fifteen LIFE-SIZE posters of *Jesus* in the halls advertising the special showing. She would also ask for permission to put flyers on each of the 500 cars in the students' parking lot. Sally made the appointment for the following Monday. (I confess my faith was small. I thought Sally and her friends would be denied permission. For though our high school principal is much more tenderhearted than Xerxes, there is enormous pressure to repress anything associated with Jesus.)

But the same God who intervened for Esther intervened for the girls.

Between Friday and Monday, God was on the move.

Sally was in a high school singing group called "The Madrigals" which had the high honor of singing at the state capital that weekend. The principal's daughter was also in "The Madrigals" and so he offered to bring the girls' long black evening dresses in his van. It happened to be snowing, causing him to run late. He quickly gathered the dresses from the dark closet, but missed *one*. It hung in the closet as he rushed to Lincoln, a two-hour drive. As the girls were dressing, they realized one of the six dresses was missing. Whose? Sally's.

The principal apologized profusely to Sally. He left two messages on our machine, telling us how badly he felt about his mistake and how gracious Sally had been.

That Monday, when Sally walked into his office for her appointment, he looked up and said, "Whatever you want, Sally. Name it."

Many many students came to Christ as a result of seeing the movie *Jesus*. Many then were discipled in small group studies.

If God be for us, who can be against us?

Prepare Your Heart to Hear

Ask God to give you something personally each day. Remember, He is there and He is not silent.

Memory Work

Perfect Esther 4:15-16:

> **Then Esther sent this reply to Mordecai: "Go, gather together all the Jews who are in Susa, and fast for me. Do not eat or drink for three days, night or day. I and my maids will fast as you do. When this is done, I will go to the king, even though it is against the law. And if I perish, I perish."**

Warm-Up

God worked in the heart of Xerxes when he could not sleep. Has God ever spoken to you during a time of insomnia or through a dream? Share briefly.

Day 1: Overview

The hard work has been done. The excitement began in Esther 5 and now escalates. The following chapters are filled with evidences of God on the move.

Go where no one can see you and dance as you sing songs of God's power such as "What a Mighty God We Serve," "Jehovah-Jirah," "He Lives," and "The Hallelujah Chorus."

1.   Comment on what stood out to you from the story in the Introductory notes (pp. 120–121).

2.   Following the first example, describe the scene as if it were in a play. Use your imagination for details and emotions.

A. Esther 6:1-3
Xerxes, reclining in his royal bed of purple satin, listens to a eunuch drone on from the book of the chronicles. Suddenly the eunuch reads of a foiled assassination attempt. Xerxes sits straight up, demanding to know what has been done for the man who saved his life. When told, "Nothing," an organ plays chords of suspense.

B. Esther 6:4-10

C. Esther 6:11

D. Esther 6:12-14

E. Esther 7:1-6

F. Esther 7:7-9

G. Esther 7:10

H. Esther 8:1-6

Detective for the Divine

How can you spy God in the above historical account?

Day 2: God on the Move

In *The Lion, the Witch, and the Wardrobe*, the Lion Aslan represents Jesus. The Witch represents Satan. As the Witch flees with her captive, Edmund, in her sleigh, a problem occurs. A thaw. Edmund begins to hope that the Witch will be foiled.

> *Every moment the patches of green grew bigger and the patches of snow grew smaller. Every moment more and more of the trees shook off their robes of snow. . . .*
>
> *Soon there were more wonderful things happening. Coming suddenly round a corner into a glade of silver birch trees Edmund saw the ground covered in all directions with little yellow flowers—celandines. . . .*
>
> *"This is no thaw," said the dwarf, suddenly stopping. "This is Spring. What are we to do? Your winter has been destroyed, I tell you! This is Aslan's doing."*
>
> *"If either of you mentions that name again," said the Witch, "he shall instantly be killed."*[75]

There is no doubt in my mind that the holocausts planned against the Jews have been engineered by Satan. But Esther and her people had fasted and prayed, and they now saw not just a thaw, but spring! God was on the move.

Read Esther 6:1-11.

3.   How can you see God on the move in Esther 6:1-3?

There is a spiritual parallel to this passage in Malachi 3:16. What is it?

4.   How can you see God on the move in Esther 6:4-5?

5.   What wrong assumption does Haman make? Describe his suggestion for "the man the king delights to honor."

The true nature of Haman is revealed in his answer. I am sure you can see what is in his heart; Haman had his eye upon the throne. It was his intention, when the time was right, to eliminate the king.
                    J. Vernon McGee[76]

6.   What evidence can you find for Haman desiring the praise of man instead of the praise of God?

Whose praise do you desire? Support your answer with evidence.

7. What "black comedy" do you see in this passage? What message is delivered through it?

8. What are some ways you have seen "God on the move" in your life?

Detective for the Divine

Have you spied God in the last twenty-four hours? If so, how?

In your personal quiet time, sing "Great Is Thy Faithfulness."

Day 3: I Will Curse Those Who Curse You

Haman, humiliated, rushed home to find comfort in the arms of his wife. She promptly told him he was finished! It was foolish, she said, to stand against the Jews! (She must have forgotten it was she who suggested a gallows be built for "that Jew Mordecai.")

Joyce Baldwin writes: "Behind this cold comfort there seems to lie commonly accepted folk wisdom, perhaps proverbial. The way the Jewish people had survived deportations and preserved their identity had not escaped notice, and this in itself witnessed to the power of their God."[77]

9. Describe how Zeresh responded to her husband's grief.

What qualities have you seen in Zeresh which would be good to avoid as a wife?

10. What do the following passages teach concerning how we should respond to the Jewish people?
    A. Genesis 12:2-3

    B. Psalm 122:6-9

11. Some might have thought that God's hand was not on the Jews beyond the borders of Israel. What does Malachi 1:1-5 teach?

12. Haman had told Xerxes that "it is not in the king's best interest to tolerate them [the Jewish people]" in Esther 3:8. How does that reveal either Haman's ignorance or failure to fear God?

13. Though many Jewish people have hardened their hearts to Jesus, God is not finished with them.

A. According to Romans 11:1-11, has God rejected His people? Have they stumbled beyond recovery?

B. What good thing has come out of the unbelief of the Jews? (Romans 11:11)

C. What warning and hope does God give to both Jews and Gentiles in Romans 11:17-24?

Day 4: Grant Me My Life

Eloquent, diplomatic, and discerning, the beautiful Esther finally made her plea.

Xerxes had repeated that she could have up to half his kingdom. Instead, she astonished him by pleading for her life!

"What is this," he thinks, "she is the queen, not some common criminal! What is she talking about?"

She clarified just how diabolical that plot was by saying, "[We] have been *sold*" (Esther 7:4). She said she would not have disturbed the king if they had just been *sold* as slaves, but since they had been *sold* for slaughter, she had come.

14. Note Esther's skill in Esther 7:1-6.

   A. How is Esther's skill shown in her timing?

   B. This time, in contrast to Esther 5:4, where she used the third person to address the king, now in 7:3 she used the second person, "you, O king." Why, do you think?

   C. Which words of the king's does she repeat in Esther 7:3? Why was it wise to repeat his words?

   D. By using the two different words the king used ("petition" and "request") she made it seem as if the king had promised her *two* favors. What is her petition? What was her request?

E. How did she reveal the depravity of the plot through her words in verse 4?

F. Where did she place the blame? Where was she careful not to place the blame?

15. What can you learn from Esther about friendly persuasion?

16. On a spiritual parallel, Esther had only recently been awakened to the peril that faced her. Likewise, many feel comfortable, secure, and unaware of the wrath to come. They have been taken captive by the enemy and are headed toward a worse fate than their slavery on earth. What are some ways you are helping others become aware of the wrath to come?

Perfect your memory passage.

Sing "And Can It Be?" or "Amazing Grace" in praise to God in your personal quiet time.

Detective for the Divine

How have you seen God in your life in the last twenty-four hours? (His Word, His Presence, His Provision)

Day 5: More God-Incidences

Haman's only hope was Esther, and while Xerxes paced the garden in a rage, Haman fell upon the queen's couch. Xerxes returned and accused Haman of molesting the queen.

D.J.A. Clines writes:

> *It simply strains credulity to believe that he actually thought that Haman under these circumstances was really attempting to assault the queen. Rather, he chooses so to interpret Haman's action, thereby providing a charge with which to condemn him that relieves the king from raising publicly the true reason for the condemnation, the plot against the Jews. Thus, in keeping with the irresponsibility that has consistently marked Ahasuerus' (Xerxes) character, he can leave hidden and unexamined his own complicity in the matter. Another remarkable coincidence has acted in favor of the Jews.*[78]

17. How do you see God on the move in Esther 7:7-10?

18. For what crime was Haman executed? What irony do you see?

19. What else does Esther reveal to the king in Esther 8:1?

Author Joy Dawson observed that neither Esther nor Mordecai could have made it alone. She likens them to being on either end of a seesaw and says the fun begins only when both partners are moving. Dawson exhorts you to be alert to the "ministry link" when God gives you a friend, for He may have a sovereign purpose in bringing her across your path.[79]

20. Think about your closest friends, husband, or an adult child. Consider if there might be a "ministry link." As you are still before God, what thoughts do you have?

21. How are the tables completely turned in Esther 8:1-2?

Detective for the Divine
Have you spied God in the last twenty-four hours? If so, how?

Day 6: How Can I Bear to See Disaster Fall on My Family?

Esther already had asked for the life of her people in Esther 7:3, but Xerxes was so preoccupied with the life of the queen that nothing was said about her people. Taking nothing for granted, Esther returned, this time weeping, falling at his feet, pleading for her people.

Again, he extended the gold scepter, the sign of favor. He listened to her carefully as she yet again diplomatically asked for something that had never been done. She wanted the laws of the Medes and Persians overturned. "For how can I bear to see disaster fall on my people? How can I bear to see the destruction of my family?" (Esther 8:6)

The spiritual parallel brings me to tears. I am so thankful that God has granted me my petition and given me my life. I am so thankful to have been rescued from the wrath to come. But I am going back to God again and again, and I am falling before Him, pleading for the lives of my loved ones. I have close family members who do not know the Lord, who seem unconcerned about the wrath to come. How can I bear to see disaster fall on my people? How can I bear to see the destruction of my family?

We have an enemy more powerful than Haman, more dangerous than Hitler. Our enemy, the devil, prowls about like a roaring lion seeking whom he may devour. Should we not come before the King of kings and pray for protection? Should we not intercede, with tears, for those Satan seeks to devour?

22. Why did Esther go back? What did she ask for?

23. What is the spiritual parallel for us?

24. What do you learn about effective intercessory prayer from the following?
    A. Psalm 51:10-14

    B. Luke 18:1-8

Personal Quiet Time

Intercede for unsaved friends and family. Write down the date, the person's name, and the prayer in a prayer journal or in the back of this guide. The following Scriptures may guide your prayers: Esther 8:6; 2 Timothy 2:25-26; and 1 Peter 3:1-17.

Detective for the Divine

Have you spied God in the last twenty-four hours? If so, how?

25. What do you think might have a lasting impact on your life from this lesson?

Prayer Time

Pair off in twos and intercede for your loved ones.

Eight

Sorrow into Joy

The Book of Esther is controversial because the story is relayed without editorial comment. So we are left to wrestle with such questions as:

Why is the book told with such restraint? Why is God's name not mentioned? Why, when we are told they fasted, are we not told if they also prayed?

Should Vashti have gone to Xerxes' drinking party? Should a woman ever defy her husband?

Should Esther have hidden her faith? Should she have slept with the king? Should she have married a pagan? Does God ever lead us into sin?

Should Mordecai have bowed to Haman? Is it ever right to show respect for an immoral leader?

I have shared the views of respected commentators on all of the above, and I have encouraged you to hold up these dark issues to the light of Christ and His Word. We should be like the Bereans, who were of noble character, and searched the Scriptures to see if what they were hearing was true (Acts 17:11). Be wary of modeling your behavior after the behavior of other believers, but always ask, "What would Jesus do?"

Now we come to the most challenging part of all, and again, commentators disagree. Was the bloodshed requested by Mordecai and Esther at the close of the book morally right?

Many commentators are quick to point out that it was not unrestrained bloodshed, that the decree sent by Esther and Mordecai gave permission only to defend themselves against anyone who "might" (in the sense of could/would/did) choose to attack. It is not permission to attack any enemy. Also, the author of Esther repeatedly tells us that no plunder was taken. These commentators believe, and they may be right, that God was working through this decree to protect the Jews. That seems to be the purpose of the wars in the Old Testament.

Chuck Swindoll compares the closing in Esther to "giving concentration camp prisoners long-overdue rights."[80] That comparison helps us to identify with the horror the Jews in Persia had been through and how glad they were to finally be able to protect themselves.

When you realize that the Jews had a whole year of waiting, anticipating the holocaust, it is logical that they might be able to discover whom their enemies were. Perhaps, God arranged the timing that way so that those with malevolent intentions would reveal themselves. (Can't you imagine it? A prejudiced Persian tells a Jewish family: "I'm going to get you on that day.") This turning of the tables, causing people to fall into the net they have set for others would be consistent with the pattern we have seen in Esther and with didactic Scriptures. (See Proverbs 1:10-19.) God may, in fact, have planned the slaughter at the close of Esther.

On the other hand, others are deeply offended by the slaughter of 75,000 boys and men. Wives were mourning for their husbands, mothers wept for their sons, and children were bereft of their fathers. F.B. Huey, Jr., in *The Expositor's Commentary*, writes: "The Jews did not limit themselves to self-defense. They hunted out and destroyed those who might harm them. . . . Could not Esther also be interpreted as another example of the postexilic failure of the Jewish people to become the exemplary people of God that He meant them to be?"[81]

Who is right? We may not know until we see Jesus face-to-face. There are some mysterious paradoxes in Scripture. I doubt we will have the answers to these paradoxes on this earth. My friend Lee Petno said, "There are two truths in Scripture that I cannot, in my limited thinking, reconcile. The first is that God cares so much for every single individual. The second is that He allows whole nations to be wiped out." The violence in the Old Testament is difficult to understand, though it seems that the wars God ordered were to protect the people from whom the Messiah would come. Was that what was happening in Esther? In the absence of editorial comment we cannot know for certain if the closing was the plan of God or the plan of man.

However, in attempting to find application to our own lives, we ourselves must decide how Jesus would have us respond to our political enemies. This too is controversial, more controversial, I believe, than the other issues we have considered in Esther. I have found believers who love the Lord to be divided on this issue. Some are very militaristic, others believe deeply in trying only peaceful solutions to political problems. I, as is true of all commentators, have an opinion which I will share. You should, like the noble Bereans, hold up what I have to say to Scripture.

As I consider history, I see that violence perpetuates violence. Though an enemy may be temporarily silenced, he plots a violent revenge, whether it is through bombs, terrorism, or chemical warfare. Peaceful solutions, on the other hand, such as have been demonstrated by Mahatma Gandhi and Martin Luther King, Jr., seem to help to stop the cycle and bring lasting results. Sometimes pacifism is defined as doing nothing, but that is a misunderstanding. These men took courageous positive actions, but not violent actions. In addition, they were willing to, and, in fact, did perish for their approaches. Esther herself demonstrated a nonviolent approach when she fasted and then went to the king to plead for her people. How often, I must ask, do Christians follow her model? Have we fallen into the world's mold in assuming that violence is our best solution?

In addition, the believers in the Old Testament did not have the words of Christ, but we do. Should we not be considering what He said when we face political problems? Daniel L. Buttrey, author of *Christian Peacemaking,* tells of a turning point in his thinking during the war in Vietnam. Buttrey had grown up in a military family and was defending the position of the United States with a college student when she asked, "If you really are serious about following Jesus, what does He say about our involvement in war?"[82] Challenged, Buttrey went back and read the New Testament with fresh eyes. Buttrey calls it his "second conversion" and went on to become a leader in the peace movement. He writes:

Jesus is the climax of biblical revelation (Hebrews 1:1-2), so rather than accepting the violence in the Old Testament as an ethical given and then trying to squeeze Jesus' teaching into that framework, we must begin with an understanding of what Jesus was saying and work our way into the rest of the Bible with a Christ-centered conceptual framework. . . . Many theological and hermeneutical approaches have undercut the lordship of Christ by subsuming Jesus' ethical teaching under a framework which minimizes or limits the scope of its impact. The attempt is made, often with great theological sophistication, to sanitize Jesus, to make Him "safe" so that the status quo will not be upset by His disturbing standards of righteousness and love. However, advocates of nonviolence and peacemaking, from the earliest days of the church to the present, find their own ethical core emerging from the core of Jesus' teaching. As a result, they have tended not to be wedded to those in power but have been voices of prophetic witness to their world and agents of social reformation.[83]

As with all controversial issues, it is important that we listen to one another with hearing ears, to consider the plumb line of Scripture, and to ask that penetrating question: "What would Jesus do?"

If we cannot agree, it is vital to listen with hearing ears, and to treat one another with respect and love. In Romans 14, Paul addressed the believers who were arguing about disputable matters. He reminded them that each would give an account to God for their choices (Romans 14:12) and so needed to be fully persuaded in their own minds (Romans 14:5). In the meantime, he exhorted them to "make every effort to do what leads to peace and to mutual edification" (Romans 14:19).

Prepare Your Heart to Hear

Ask God to give you His discernment as you study, each day.

Memory Work

Review Romans 11:33 and Esther 4:12-16. Review these each year during holy week (the week that Haman threw the Pur, the week of Passover, the week of Easter) and you will have them forever.

Warm-Up

What did you find most controversial in Esther? How did you resolve the controversy in the light of Christ and His Word?

Day 1: Overview

Imagine the relief! The day in which they and their children are to be slaughtered hangs over the Jews like a dark cloud. The last time the king's horses raced out it was to post that terrible edict. What is it this time? Woodrow Kroll imagines the Jews crowding around the posted signs with dread. And then! Cries of astonished relief, weeping, and embracing of loved ones.[84] It is a wonderful picture, as J. Vernon McGee points out, of us and our great salvation.[85] Doomed to the wrath of God, we have been set free by a new edict, the grace made possible through our Lord Jesus Christ.

Begin your personal quiet time with Billy Graham's favorite hymn: "And Can It Be?"

1.   Comment on what stood out to you from the Introductory notes (pp. 135–138).

Read Esther 8:7-10:3.

2.   As you read, identify with the Jews. Describe their emotions and actions.

Spend five minutes reviewing your memory passages.

3.   When believers disagree on gray issues such as methods of raising children, styles of worship, and political solutions, what should be their attitude according to Romans 14:10-12?

4.   What gray issues have caused disagreement between you and another believer? What could you do to be at peace with her?

Detective for the Divine
Have you seen God at work in your life in the last twenty-four hours? If so, how?

Day 2: The Royal Horses Raced Out

The laws of the Medes and the Persians cannot be changed. Frederic Bush says that in the Hebrew the use of the emphasizing particle shows an exasperated tone. Xerxes' attitude in Esther 8:7 is: "Look at what I have done for you! I have hanged Haman and given you his estate—what more do you want?"[86] Xerxes was not concerned with the slaughter of the Jews, but Esther's diplomacy had prevailed and, giving in, Xerxes took off his signet ring and, in characteristic irresponsibility, gave Esther and Mordecai the power to do whatever they chose.

Esther deferred to Mordecai, who wrote a new order, turning the tables. The Jews could assemble, protect themselves, and annihilate any armed force that might attack them. The couriers raced out on royal chariot horses to post the new edict.

Read Esther 8:7-14.

5.   What authority does Xerxes give Esther and Mordecai? (Esther 8:7-8)

6.   Compare Esther 3:13-15 with Esther 8:9-10. What similarities do you see? What differences?

7.   Describe the new edict (Esther 8:11).

The Hebrew in 8:11 is difficult and some think it means the Jews could kill women and children and take the plunder. Joyce Baldwin considers that the phrase "women and children" is the object of the verb attack.[87] In other words, the Jews could kill anyone who might have attacked their women and children and plundered their property.

8. Describe the joyful scene in Esther 8:15-17.

How do you think you would feel if you were a Jew experiencing this? Explain.

9. Has there been a time in your life when you expected the worst and then received unexpected grace? Can you identify with this spiritually? If so, explain.

10. What reaction do many of other nationalities have? (Esther 8:17)

Why do you think they thought it might be advantageous to be Jewish? Do you think they were sincere or nominal Jews? Explain.

Are you a Christian because of the advantages? If your faith were tested, you lost everything, would you still cling to God?

Detective for the Divine

Have you grown in your love of God in the last twenty-four hours? If so, how?

Day 3: Relief from Their Enemies

The bloodshed was enormous. Five hundred were killed in the citadel. Then the ten sons of Haman were killed.

Is it enough? Xerxes asked Esther if she was satisfied. She asked for the bodies of Haman's sons to be displayed and a second day of killing. Three hundred more were killed in Susa and 75,000 in the provinces of Persia.

In my opinion, I think Esther is still deferring to Mordecai. This request sounds suspiciously like Mordecai, to whom Esther has always deferred. It was Mordecai's hatred of the Agagites which precipitated the situation in the first place. I would agree with F.B. Huey, Jr. who asks, "If Esther and Mordecai had forgiven their enemies instead of demanding vengeance, would God have been pleased and protected His people?"[88] Huey also asks if possibly God's silence in the Book of Esther could be "interpreted as evidence that the people were working out their own affairs without consulting Him. There is no historical evidence that the Jewish people entered into a period of blessing after the events of Esther, a blessing that might have been expected if God were guiding their actions (Deut. 28)."[89]

11. Describe what happened on the first day in which the tables were turned (Esther 9:1-10).

12. What else does Esther request? (Esther 9:11-13)

13. Describe what happened on the second day (Esther 9:14-17).

14. What do you learn about responding to our enemies from the following?
    A. Matthew 5:38-48

    B. Matthew 26:50-52

    C. Romans 12:17-21

15. Are you facing evil in your life? How could you overcome it with good?

16. How do you view the measures the Jews took to gain relief from their enemies in Esther? Why?

Review your memory work.

Detective for the Divine
Have you seen God at work in your life in the last twenty-four hours? If so, how?

Day 4: Mourning into a Day of Celebration

Mordecai and Esther established a celebration to commemorate the month when "their sorrow was turned into joy and their mourning into a day of celebration" (Esther 9:22). Frederic Bush points out that Purim is understood to be a reference to "pur," the lot cast by Haman. Therefore "the very name of the festival itself brings to mind neither military victory nor the slaughter of enemies, but Haman's plot and their subsequent deliverance from evil and disaster."[90]

Traditions were established for Purim, and I see Esther's hand. For example, in Esther 9:31, days of fasting were to precede the days of feasting. I think this was to commemorate Esther's fast, when God anointed her with wisdom and power. Also, in Esther 9:19 and 9:22, during the days of feasting, presents of food were to be given to one another, and also gifts sent to the poor. Joyce Baldwin likens it to the child who comes back from a party with a choice morsel wrapped in a napkin for one who is special to him. Baldwin, drawing upon some research by Sandra Beth Berg, illuminates a deeper meaning in this particular tradition. I think these two distinguished women are right, and to me it illumines not only the custom of sending portions, but Esther's faith. So read this carefully!

In the KJV, Esther 9:19 is translated "portions one to another," and, again, in Esther 9:22, "sending portions one to another, and gifts to the poor." This same word is used in Psalm 16:5 when the Lord is called our "portion" and Psalm 16:6 goes on to say "The lines are fallen unto me in pleasant places." Baldwin says:

> Here the "lot" or "portion" is an allusion to the way life has worked out; the psalmist is thinking of all the signs of God's providence which have marked his pilgrimage, and which unbelievers think of as "fate." It would not be surprising, therefore, if the word had within it suggestions of destiny. Within the context of Esther's receipt of portions from Hegai, the special favors she receives anticipate the king's later reaction to her. . . . At the end of the story, when festivities mark the reversal of Jewish fortunes from the threat of death to life and favour, the exchange of "portions" is especially appropriate. The sending of "portions" often signified special favour and . . . suitably characterizes the celebration of the feast of "lots."[91]

Read Esther 9:18-32.

17. What was the purpose of Purim according to 9:22?

18. Why was it called Purim? (Esther 9:24)

What link do you see between the name "Purim" and God's providence?

19. In Esther 9:19 and 9:22 they were to send "portions" to each other. Have you observed the tradition of bringing a "portion" from a party or a holiday home to someone? What message does that convey?

20. In Psalm 16:5-6, how is this word "portion" used?

How can you see that God's favor was on Esther, that He made "her lot secure"?

21. What other tradition was established in Esther 9:31? What would this bring to mind?

22. How lasting was this celebration to be and why? (Esther 9:27-28)

23. How did God continue to protect His people in Persia? (Esther 10:3)

Frederic Bush points out that Hitler, unlike Haman, was successful in eliminating six million Jews. For those Jews there was no Esther. He writes: "Faith hardly knows how to hang on to the providence of God in such circumstances—but it must." For this reason, Bush reflects, the Book of Esther and the celebration of Purim become especially important, summoning the community to hold onto its faith and its hope.[92]

24. Can you share a time when God turned your sorrow into joy?

Today a birth announcement arrived from missionary friends, Travis and Susan Stewart, who years ago suffered the death of their long-awaited and only child, a newborn boy. On the birth announcement was a picture of their daughter, Laura Joy, and Esther 9:22: "Sorrow was turned into joy and their mourning into a day of celebration."

25. When life is difficult for you, what evidence can you look back to that reminds you of God's love and care?

Detective for the Divine

Have you seen God at work in your life in the last twenty-four hours? If so, how?

Day 5: Celebrations Which Honor God

Purim is still observed by many of the Jewish faith. A festival held yearly in the streets of Tel Aviv is attended by thousands. In keeping with the satirical spirit of Esther, there is little decorum and much merriment, somewhat like Halloween or New Year's Eve. Children wear costumes and paint their faces. The Book of Esther is read and the children blow noisemakers when Haman's name is read and cheer at the names of Mordecai and Esther. Portions of food are sent to friends, the most popular being "Haman's pockets" which are three-cornered pies.[93] There are three prayers offered at Purim: they thank Jehovah they are counted worthy; they thank Him for preserving their ancestors; and they thank Him they have lived to see another festival.[94]

Purim was established, not by God, but by Mordecai and Esther, yet that does not mean it cannot honor God. It can be a time when people reflect on the reality of God and His care, or it can simply be a time to eat, drink, and be merry. Our holidays of Thanksgiving, Christmas, and Easter were established by believers and not by God, yet they can honor God. However, for many they have become simply times to eat, drink, and be merry.

Holiday traditions can teach our children about God. The high point of our Thanksgiving occurs when each person at the table gives thanks for something he or she could not have been thankful for the previous year. The Christmas carols are filled with vital doctrines and we should be singing them together in our cars and in our homes. Fasting on Good Friday, or even the giving up of candy during Lent, can be reminders of what Christ gave up for us. Likewise, Easter baskets laden with jelly beans can be a reminder of God's goodness. (This tradition reminds me of the fast and feast of Purim.) However, traditions can easily be passed on without their meaning—a form of godliness without the power. The real secret to meaningful holidays is getting our hearts right with God. The rest will follow, for the way that we celebrate is a reflection of our hearts.

26. Think about your recent celebrations of holidays. How did those times reflect your ardor (or lack of it) for God?

Read Nehemiah 8:5-12.

Nehemiah is a story of revival and Ezra is the priest who led the revival. The people wept in repentance as Ezra read from God's Word. Then Nehemiah led them in a celebration which is similar to the celebration we see described in the close of Esther.

27. What instructions did Nehemiah and the Levite priests give to the people? (Nehemiah 8:9-12)

What similarities do you see with Purim?

Do you see any of the holiday customs of Nehemiah or Esther reflected in customs of Thanksgiving, Christmas, or Easter?

Read Isaiah 1:10-20.

28. Why did God hate the festivals and celebrations of the Israelites?

What did He long to see in their lives?

Read Isaiah 58.

29. Why was God not pleased with the fasts of the Israelites?

What did He long to see in their lives?

Detective for the Divine

Have you grown in your understanding of God and His ways in the last twenty-four hours? If so, how?

Day 6: Reflecting on Esther

Though the Book of Esther occurred twenty-five centuries ago, the struggles against sin and Satan sound just like the struggles of our day. We live in a world of pride and prejudice, of vanity and violence. We live in a world in which even our leaders and often the people who call themselves believers are obsessed with sexual immorality, entertainment, and materialism. Often God seems strangely silent.

We live in a world in desperate need of revival.

Revival begins with the individual. Esther gives us the opportunity to reflect on the state of our own heart.

Review
Begin your quiet time by singing: "Immortal, Invisible" and "In His Time."

ONE: PROVIDENCE
Give evidence from the Book of Esther that God had not forsaken His people, even though they may have been far from Him.

TWO: THE TIDES OF THE TIMES
Review the opening chapter of Esther and describe the tides of the times.

One of the best ways to determine the state of our heart is to consider what we think about, dream about, and how we spend our time. Where is your heart?

THREE: THE CONTEST FOR THE NEW MISS PERSIA
Often believers try to accomplish God's work by doing things the way the world does. How can you see this in Esther 2?

As you examine your ministries for the Lord, are you approaching them His way or the world's way?

FOUR: DARKNESS AND DESPAIR, BUT GOD STILL REIGNS
Suffering can be a result of many things—both the righteous and the wicked suffer. But when suffering comes, it is always good to examine our hearts and to see if there is any wicked way in us. What do you think might have been the cause of suffering in Esther 3?

As you are still before God, is there any wicked way in you?

FIVE: PREDICAMENT, PRIVILEGE, AND PROVIDENCE
Explain how Esther 4:12-14 highlights these themes.

Consider the privileges God has given you and how seriously you are approaching them.

SIX: OUT OF THE COCOON OF CRISIS EMERGES A BUTTERFLY
Describe Esther's stand in Esther 4:15-16.

Have you come to an "If I perish, I perish" understanding of life?

SEVEN: IF GOD BE FOR US, WHO CAN BE AGAINST US?
How did God seem to give Esther wisdom and power in Esther 5–8?

What did you learn from Esther concerning approaching difficult situations?

EIGHT: SORROW INTO JOY
What did you see in the close of Esther that you believe was either pleasing or displeasing to God?

As you examine the way you celebrate holidays, what improvements might you make?

Ask God to show you what is most important for you to take away, right now, from the Book of Esther. Put it in one, at most two, concise sentences.

Prayer Time
Based on what you have shared in the last question, pray for one another, that God will etch this truth in your heart so that your life will be different.

Sources

Introduction

1. F.B. Huey, Jr., "Esther." The Expositor's Bible Commentary. Vol. 4. Ed. Frank E. Gaebelein and Richard P. Polcyn (Grand Rapids: Zondervan, 1988), 793.
2. John F. Brug, People's Commentary Bible: Ezra Nehemiah Esther (St. Louis: C.P.H., 1985), 155–56.

One: Providence

3. "Providence." Unger's Bible Dictionary (Chicago: Moody, 1966), 897.
4. Francis Schaeffer, He Is There and He Is Not Silent (Wheaton: Tyndale, 1972), n.p.
5. Corrie ten Boom with John and Elizabeth Sherrill, The Hiding Place (Old Tappan, New Jersey: Fleming, 1971), 176.
6. Billy Graham, Just As I Am: The Autobiography of Billy Graham (New York: HarperCollins, 1997), 24.
7. Joni Eareckson Tada, Secret Strength (Portland: Multnomah, 1988), 162
8. J. Vernon McGee, Ezra, Nehemiah, and Esther (Nashville: Thomas Nelson, 1991), 170.
9. "Cyrus." Unger's Bible Dictionary, 233.
10. F.B. Huey, Jr., "Esther." The Expositor's Bible Commentary, 786.

Two: The Tides of the Times

11. C.S. Lewis, The Weight of Glory (Grand Rapids: Eerdmans, 1965), 1–2.
12. J. Vernon McGee, Ezra, Nehemiah, and Esther, 176.
13. J.G. McConville, Ezra, Nehemiah, and Esther (Philadelphia: Westminster, 1985), 156.
14. Flavius Josephus, "The Antiquities of the Jews." Josephus: Complete Works. trans. by William Whiston (Grand Rapids: Kregel, 1981), 237.
15. Jonathan ben Uzziel, as quoted in Adam Clark, "Esther." Clark's Commentary (Nashville: Abingdon, n.d.), 808.
16. Joyce G. Baldwin, Esther: An Introduction and Commentary (Downers Grove, Ill.: IVP, 1984), 55–56.
17. W. Dinwiddie, "The Book of Esther." The Pulpit Commentary. Vol. 7. Ed. H.D.M. Spence and Joseph S. Exell (Peabody, Mass.: Hendrickson, n.d.), 29.
18. Joni Eareckson Tada, When God Weeps: Why Our Sufferings Matter to the Almighty (Grand Rapids: Zondervan, 1997), 41–45.
19. F.B. Huey, Jr., "Esther." The Expositor's Bible Commentary, 799.
20. Ibid.
21. Woodrow Kroll, "Living Courageously in Difficult Times." Back to the Bible, 1997.
22. John F. Brug, People's Commentary Bible: Ezra Nehemiah Esther, 166.
23. F.B. Huey, Jr., "Esther." The Expositor's Bible Commentary, 789.
24. Ibid.
25. Elizabeth Rice Handford, Me! Obey Him? (Murfreesboro, Tenn.: Sword of the Lord, 1972), 57.
26. J. Vernon McGee, Ezra, Nehemiah, and Esther, 180.
27. Charles R. Swindoll, A Woman of Strength & Dignity: Esther (Nashville: Word, 1997), 27.
28. Dr. Henry Cloud and Dr. John Townsend, Boundaries (Grand Rapids: Zondervan, 1992), 161–62.

Three: The Contest for the New Miss Persia

29. Frederic W. Bush, "Esther." Word Biblical Commentary. Vol. 9. Ed. David A. Hubbard, Glenn W. Barker and John D.W. Watts (Dallas: Word, 1996), 315–16.
30. W. Clarkson, "The Book of Esther." The Pulpit Commentary, 54.
31. Pastor John Bronson, Guest Speaker's Sermon to the Evangelical Free Church of Kearney, Neb. June 1986.
32. John F. Brug, People's Commentary Bible: Ezra Nehemiah Esther, 166.
33. "Life Visits Mrs. Bunny." Life, September 1989: 108.
34. Joyce G. Baldwin, The New Bible Commentary Revised. Ed. D.G. Guthrie and J.A. Motyer (Grand Rapids: Eerdman's, 1970), 415.
35. Flavius Josephus, "The Antiquities of the Jews." Josephus: Complete Works, 238.
36. Paton, as quoted in Joyce G. Baldwin, Esther: An Introduction and Commentary, 66.
37. F.B. Huey, Jr., "Esther." The Expositor's Bible Commentary, 804.
38. Frederic W. Bush, "Esther." Word Biblical Commentary, 367.
39. Carl Armerding, Esther: For Such a Time As This (Chicago: Moody, 1955), 40.
40. J. Vernon McGee, Ezra, Nehemiah, and Esther, 190.
41. Joyce G. Baldwin, Esther: An Introduction and Commentary, 66.
42. Jamieson, Fausset and Brown, as quoted in Carl Armerding, Esther: For Such a Time As This, 24.
43. Joyce G. Baldwin, Esther: An Introduction and Commentary, 68.
44. Carl Armerding, Esther: For Such a Time As This, 24–25, 29.
45. Alexis de Tocqueville, as quoted in Susan Hunt, The True Woman: The Beauty of Strength of a Godly Woman (Wheaton: Crossway, 1997), 21.
46. David Wells, as quoted in Susan Hunt, The True Woman: The Beauty of Strength of a Godly Woman, 23.
47. D. Rowlands, "The Book of Esther." The Pulpit Commentary, 58.

48. Joyce G. Baldwin, *Esther: An Introduction and Commentary*, 67–68.

49. Frederic W. Bush, "Esther." *Word Biblical Commentary*, 365.

50. D. Rowlands, "The Book of Esther." *The Pulpit Commentary*, 58.

Four: Darkness and Despair, but God Still Reigns

51. Frederic W. Bush, "Esther." *Word Biblical Commentary*, 384.

52. Woodrow Kroll, "Living Courageously in Difficult Days." Back to the Bible, 1997.

53. Frederic W. Bush, "Esther." *Word Biblical Commentary*, 379.

54. J. Vernon McGee, *Ezra, Nehemiah, and Esther*, 198.

55. John C. Whitcomb, *Esther: Triumph of God's Sovereignty* (Chicago: Moody, 1979), 66.

Five: Predicament, Privilege, and Providence

56. Elizabeth Dole, "Crisis and Faith." *Finding God at Harvard* (Grand Rapids: Zondervan, 1996), n.p.

57. Ibid., 241.

58. Ibid., 242.

59. Ibid.

60. Charles R. Swindoll, "Esther." Insight for Living, 1989.

61. Joyce G. Baldwin, *Esther: An Introduction and Commentary*, 76.

62. Frederic W. Bush, "Esther." *Word Biblical Commentary*, 398.

63. Joyce G. Baldwin, *Esther: An Introduction and Commentary*, 77.

64. Ibid., 80.

65. J. Vernon McGee, *Ezra, Nehemiah, and Esther*, 213.

66. Frederic W. Bush, "Esther." *Word Biblical Commentary*, 396.

67. Charles R. Swindoll, *A Woman of Strength & Dignity: Esther*, 4.

Six: Out of the Cocoon of Crisis Emerges a Butterfly

68. Joni Eareckson Tada, "Life Is Hard . . . But God Is Good." Address to Moody Bible Institute during Founders Week. Chicago. 7 Feb. 1998.

69. C.S. Lewis, *The Lion, the Witch and the Wardrobe* (New York: Harper Trophy, 1978), 85–86.

70. Bill Bright, *The Coming Revival: America's Call to Fast, Pray, and "Seek God's Face"* (Orlando: New Life, 1995), 60.

71. Woodrow Kroll, "Living Courageously During Difficult Days." Back to the Bible, 1997.

72. Charles R. Swindoll, *A Woman of Strength & Dignity: Esther*, 96.

73. Brenda Wilbee, *Taming the Dragons: Christian Women Resolving Conflict* (New York: HarperSanFrancisco, 1992), 58.

74. D.J.A. Clines, as quoted in Frederic W. Bush, "Esther." *Word Biblical Commentary*, 407.

Seven: If God Be for Us, Who Can Be against Us?

75. C.S. Lewis, *The Lion, the Witch and the Wardrobe*, 131, 133.

76. J. Vernon McGee, *Ezra, Nehemiah, and Esther*, 226.

77. Joyce G. Baldwin, *Esther: An Introduction and Commentary*, 91.

78. D.J.A. Clines, as quoted in Frederic W. Bush, "Esther." *Word Biblical Commentary*, 433.

79. Joy Dawson, "Team Ministry." Address to a Leadership Conference. Seattle. March 1988.

Eight: Sorrow into Joy

80. Charles R. Swindoll, *A Woman of Strength & Dignity: Esther*, 158.

81. F.B. Huey, Jr., "Esther." *The Expositor's Bible Commentary*, 787, 833.

82. Daniel L. Buttrey, *Christian Peacemaking* (Valley Forge, Pa.: Judson Press, 1984), 6–8.

83. Ibid.

84. Woodrow Kroll, "Living Courageously During Difficult Days." Back to the Bible, 1997.

85. J. Vernon McGee, *Ezra, Nehemiah, and Esther*, 238.

86. Frederic W. Bush, "Esther." *Word Biblical Commentary*, 452.

87. Joyce G. Baldwin, *Esther: An Introduction and Commentary*, 98.

88. F.B. Huey, Jr., "Esther." *The Expositor's Bible Commentary*, 787.

89. Ibid.

90. Frederic W. Bush, "Esther." *Word Biblical Commentary*, 329.

91. Joyce G. Baldwin, *Esther: An Introduction and Commentary*, 112–13.

92. Frederic W. Bush, "Esther." *Word Biblical Commentary*, 331.

93. Ibid., 330.

94. J. Vernon McGee, *Ezra, Nehemiah, and Esther*, 246.

A Personal Note From the Author

Heart

Many of you have written to me through my website. Esther has shown you that God is the God of second chances, and that He can still use you though you've failed Him in the past. I know many of you have wounded hearts. May this study bring healing and give you hope that He can still use you mightily.

Soul

How I identify with Esther pleading for the lives of her people. We have an enemy more powerful than Haman, more dangerous than Hitler. Our enemy prowls around like a roaring lion, seeking whom he may devour. Every day I go to my King and plead for the souls of my loved ones, especially for the soul of my eighty-seven-year-old father. We must fast and pray.

> For how can I bear to see disaster fall on my people?
> How can I bear to see the destruction of my family? (Esther 8:6)

Mind

Esther is the most challenging book on which I've written a study guide. Letters have poured in that show me how you are thinking, turning these verses over in your mind. I thank God for that, and I pray that you will be like the Bereans, who examined the Word every day to see if what they were being taught was true (Acts 17:11). For additional reading, consider the Sources in the back of the book, especially the academic sources, which go back to the Hebrew.

Strength

I saw my own daughter and her friends follow the example of Esther in order to be used mightily of God in their high school. How exciting it was to see God on the move. Our strength is in Him, and if He is for us, who can be against us?

Father,
May my sister, like Esther, be willing to perish to her own agenda and then see You use her mightily. In the powerful name of Jesus, Amen.